# THE 88 RULES OF WEALTH

Easy lessons on building and keeping wealth

Mia Galgau

## Opening Critique

Some books on money bury you in spreadsheets and statistics. Others dive so deep into psychology that they float away from real life. Every once in a while, though, a book manages to connect the two—showing not only how wealth comes together but also why it so often slips through our fingers, gets distorted, or disappears altogether.

*The 88 Rules of Wealth* doesn't sell shortcuts or formulas. It acts as both a mirror and a compass. The mirror reflects the patterns that have shaped wealth for centuries, and the compass points to principles sturdy enough to outlast markets, governments, or passing trends. Each rule works like a story with a lesson tucked inside, reminding us that money is rarely about genius and almost always about habits.

What makes these pages different is their candor. There's no promise of full control, no dismissal of envy, fear, or greed as if they could be erased. The point is to show how to live alongside them, to build systems stronger than moods, and to turn consistency into genuine independence. The truth isn't sugar-coated: the hardest task in finance is simply staying in the game long enough for compounding to work in your favor.

Readers won't find hype here. What they'll find is perspective. They'll see why saving cautiously but investing with optimism isn't a contradiction at all, but a kind of wisdom. Why reputation can be more valuable than a pile of cash. Why governments always protect themselves first, why families are both central and fragile, and why legacy is less about monuments than about continuity.

More than anything, they'll see themselves in these rules. Because wealth is not an abstract idea–it's human. It's the daily tug-of-war between desire and fear, between what lies within our reach and what we simply have to endure. By the time the last rule is read, the aim isn't just to understand wealth but to know how to use it, how to build independence deliberately, and how to create something that lasts beyond your own lifetime.

This isn't a book for skimming. It's meant to stay close, to be reread, argued with, and applied. It's a reminder of something easy to overlook: money is not the destination. Freedom is. And freedom, as these pages insist, is never handed over–it's something you design.

# The 88 Rules of Wealth

**Building Wealth (Rules 1–20)**

1. Save before you spend
2. Live below your means, but not below your dignity
3. Compounding is invisible until it manifests
4. Own assets, not just income
5. Invest in what you understand
6. Diversify, but don't dilute
7. Cash flow is king
8. Turn skills into capital
9. Build multiple income streams
10. Leverage technology, not just labor
11. Use debt sparingly—and only as leverage, never as lifestyle
12. Learn to read balance sheets
13. Taxes are the biggest hidden expense
14. Automate savings and investments
15. Negotiate everything
16. Insurance is protection, not investment
17. Protect downside before chasing upside
18. Build assets that pay while you sleep
19. Keep liquidity for crises and opportunities
20. A small win repeated beats a windfall wasted

**Foundations (Rules 21–35)**

21. Wealth is not money
22. Enough is a moving target
23. Freedom is the ultimate currency
24. Protect before you grow
25. Reputation is capital
26. Risk is the price of reward
27. Luck is part of every fortune
28. Simplicity beats complexity
29. Control is more valuable than income
30. Inflation is the silent thief
31. Expenses define you more than income
32. Wealth without purpose is emptiness
33. Paper beats memory
34. Systems survive mood swings
35. The story you tell yourself matters most

**Human Psychology (Rules 36–53)**

36. Fear sells faster than hope

37. Greed never sleeps
38. Envy destroys silently
39. Loss feels twice as heavy as gain
40. The crowd is usually wrong
41. Timing is luck, not genius
42. Patience is the hardest investment
43. Confidence without discipline is ruin
44. Certainty is an illusion
45. FOMO is the modern tax
46. People remember stories, not numbers
47. The bigger the ego, the weaker the fortress
48. Security feels boring until you lose it
49. Shortcuts cost more in the end
50. Stress compounds faster than money
51. Happiness has no market price
52. Scarcity creates value
53. Trust is a currency

**Structures and Systems (Rules 54–73)**

54. Laws change, principles endure
55. Borders define opportunity
56. Paperwork is power
57. Privacy is protection
58. Diversification is survival
59. Complexity hides risk
60. Offshore is structure, not escape
61. Jurisdictional arbitrage beats speculation
62. Every system has gatekeepers
63. Rules multiply in crisis
64. Governments protect themselves first
65. Transparency has limits
66. Bureaucracy outlives regimes
67. Data is property
68. Institutions remember longer than individuals
69. Leverage magnifies both gains and losses
70. Liquidity is oxygen
71. Contracts are weapons
72. Family is the most fragile structure
73. Advisors serve their own interests first

**Practice and Discipline (Rules 74–83)**

74. Save like a pessimist, invest like an optimist
75. Automatic beats emotional

# Introduction

Advice fades. Rules endure.

This book isn't a collection of quick financial tips to chase during the next boom or bust. It's a map of patterns that stretch beyond the moment, principles that matter whether you're just opening your first savings account, managing a company, or preparing to pass down a fortune.

Wealth isn't a finish line. It isn't a number printed on a statement or some trophy to display. It's a rhythm—the steady beat of choices made over years, the balance between what you earn, what you keep, and what you truly value. Some rules may feel counterintuitive, others almost too obvious, yet each one matters. Because money, at its core, has never been about math alone. It's always been about behavior.

These pages are written for anyone who's felt both the promise and the burden of money. For the young professional who discovers that saving is harder than earning. For the business owner who realizes that growth can invite fragility. For the investor who's seen markets move faster than discipline. And for the parent or grandparent who understands that passing on wealth without passing on meaning can be more dangerous than leaving nothing at all.

The rules here aren't theories. They are the distillation of centuries—most of it failure, a smaller share hard-won success. You'll learn why compounding feels dull until suddenly it's unstoppable, why debt so often wears the mask of freedom, and why simplicity has a way of outperforming complexity. You'll see how reputation becomes a form of capital, why freedom is the only currency that matters in the end, and how legacies crumble when there's no purpose to sustain them.

Some lessons will reassure. Others may sting. That contrast is intentional. Wealth is full of contradictions. It promises freedom yet creates pressure. It protects and exposes. It can nurture dynasties or tear families apart. Grasping those paradoxes is far more important than memorizing formulas.

The 88 rules that follow trace a journey most people will recognize. They begin with the mechanics of building—saving, investing, structuring. From there, they explore the foundations that give wealth meaning. Then comes psychology, the invisible battlefield where fear, envy, and impatience undo even the strongest balance sheet. After that, the lens widens to systems and structures—laws, governments, institutions that shape the terrain. Finally, the path turns to practice, discipline, continuity, and legacy, because money that cannot outlive its owner was never wealth at all.

You won't find shortcuts here. Nor will you find secret formulas that guarantee riches. What you will find are frameworks that have survived speculation, bubbles, and entire eras. Rules that explain why some hold on to wealth while others let it slip away. Rules that help you build with clarity, protect with foresight, and leave behind something more lasting than money itself.

If you read this book as a manual, you'll miss its purpose. Read it as a mirror. Each rule reflects the choices you already make, the habits you already live. Some will affirm what you know deep down. Others will reveal blind spots you never noticed. Together, they will remind you that wealth isn't a sprint toward "more." It's a rhythm—and rhythm is what keeps you steady when the world speeds up.

# Rule 1 – Save before you spend

Wealth usually begins with a decision so small it almost feels invisible. It isn't tied to picking the right stock or striking a clever deal. It's about the order in which you handle the very first dollar that lands in your account. Most people spend first and then try to save whatever scraps remain. It sounds harmless–until you notice how life is designed to make sure there's never anything left over. Paydays seem to come with new "needs" that appear right on schedule. Flipping the sequence–saving first, then spending what remains–doesn't feel dramatic in the moment, but it rewires the entire story of your money.

The power isn't in the size of the amount; it's in the priority. Ten dollars set aside before you touch anything else beats a hundred you manage to keep only when the month goes well. Saving first turns tomorrow into a bill you pay as seriously as rent or electricity. What matters here isn't math–it's psychology. Math compounds only on what your behavior allows to survive. Each time you save first, you're making a quiet statement: *I pay my future self before I pay the world.* That identity sticks. Once you adopt it, it defends itself on the days your discipline wears thin.

This doesn't require heroic willpower. It requires design. If money has to pass through your hands before heading to savings, it will leak. Automating the transfer–sending part of your income straight into a separate account you don't scroll past every day–removes mood from the equation. Consistency becomes automatic, and automatic is where compounding hides. The goal isn't to prove how spartan you can be.

The goal is to make the right thing happen by default, especially on the days you're busy, tired, or distracted.

The weakness of "I'll save what's left" is easy to underestimate. The month you plan for is never the month you actually get. A car breaks down, a friend visits, a sale tempts you, or a headline pushes you to buy something unnecessary. If saving comes last, it's the shock absorber for every surprise. If it comes first, everything else has to fit into what's left. That repeated constraint is how wealth sneaks up on people who never felt rich while they were building it.

Here's a useful way to think about it: guaranteed versus speculative returns. Every dollar you don't spend gives you a certain 100% improvement in net worth compared to spending it. The investment you hope will double remains just a hope until it does. Saving is not the destination–it's the fuel that lets you invest–but the certainty of saving first gives you the right to take risk later without turning volatility into a crisis. Markets pay unevenly. Bills arrive on time. Saving first is how you keep bills from dictating your investment strategy.

Some people argue inflation makes saving pointless. That confuses cash with saving. Saving is not a vow to sit on cash. It's a vow to create a surplus. That surplus is the raw material you can deploy into cash for stability, bonds for ballast, equities for growth, a business for cash flow, or a down payment that erases a rent bill. Saving first creates the surplus. What you do with it is strategy. One is behavior. The other is allocation. Without the first, the second doesn't exist.

There's also the treadmill problem. If you spend first, every raise feeds lifestyle inflation. Each upgrade becomes the new baseline, and the treadmill speeds up. Saving first breaks that cycle. Raises accelerate freedom instead of inflating lifestyle. The spread between income and expenses—the gap—is what drives independence. Saving first forces that gap to exist and keeps it alive. Resilience comes not from earning more, but from widening and preserving that spread when the world grows noisy.

Picture two colleagues earning the same salary. One spends first and occasionally saves what's left—usually nothing. The other saves a fixed percentage the morning income arrives. For years, little seems different. Then a downturn hits, interest rates jump, or a family expense explodes out of nowhere. The spender scrambles, forced to make choices under pressure. The saver has a buffer. That buffer buys time, and time buys good decisions. When markets recover, both say they learned something. Only one has the capital to use the lesson.

Saving first is not austerity. It's priority. You are free to spend afterward. The rhythm is what matters. That rhythm allows generosity without fear and indulgence without guilt, because the future has already been paid. It lets you ignore financial noise and skip having an opinion on every forecast. Your savings habit makes you immune to all that.

If this rule had to live in a single line, it would be this: treat your future as your most relentless creditor and pay that bill first, every time. The rest of life will adjust around that constraint. A decade later, people may call it luck. But it wasn't luck. It was sequence. You changed the order of operations and gave time the chance to reward those who showed up early.

## Rule 2 – Live below your means, but not below your dignity

Frugality often drifts into performance. Some people wear it like a badge, convinced virtue is measured by how little they can get by with. Others flaunt the opposite, using spending as a loud broadcast of status. Both are illusions—the kind the future plays on the present. The real point of living below your means isn't sainthood, and it isn't spectacle. It's margin. Room in your life so that surprises don't break you and opportunities don't slip past. At the same time, living above your dignity keeps the confidence alive that makes restraint sustainable for more than a brief season.

Living below your means buys you options, and options are the real luxury. A cushion lets you walk away from a toxic boss, decline a client whose money twists your values, or take a sabbatical when your mind frays. It lets you hold cash through a downturn without liquidating assets you love at prices you hate. Margin is rarely exciting—until the day after it saves you. Then it becomes the one thing you crave more of. The mistake comes when people chase margin by attacking their own self-respect. They confuse being cheap with being wise, or shame with discipline. That works for a while, and then it collapses.

Dignity isn't about a marble foyer or a watch with a Swiss pedigree. It's the basics that preserve your sense of self. The mattress that lets you sleep. The dentist appointment you don't delay under the excuse of "being frugal." Shoes that don't injure your feet. A laptop that won't crash when your work is due. A meal with friends you can accept without resentment gnawing in the background. If the way you live beneath your means makes you feel small, sooner or later you'll rebel–loudly, and expensively. Deprivation doesn't disappear; it rebounds.

Sustainable restraint is quiet and selective. It trims where trimming compounds: subscriptions you don't value, square footage you never use, cars that signal more than they serve, upgrades that create habits without real utility. It spends on what stabilizes your life and expands your ability to earn and think. The question isn't "is this the cheapest option," but "does this reduce fragility or increase it." A bargain tool that fails at the worst time isn't a bargain. An indulgence that hardens into a fixed cost is not a reward; it's a leash.

Here's a test: would your thoughtful future self be embarrassed to see how you live now? Not embarrassed by the absence of luxury, but by the absence of care. Eating poorly, sleeping poorly, isolating yourself in the name of discipline–none of that is discipline. It's sabotage that eventually shows up as missed opportunities and brittle decisions. Confidence is compound interest on self-respect. You invest small amounts in it every day, and over time, you act from calm rather than scarcity.

Context complicates everything. In circles where wealth is performed, indulgence becomes normal. In circles where minimalism is worshipped, denial becomes normal. Anchors shape what "enough" looks like. Change your room, change your anchor. One of the most underrated financial decisions is choosing company that doesn't constantly drag your baseline upward or downward. The quiet middle–where money serves life instead of theater–is easier to live in when the people around you are looking for it too.

Living below your means while protecting your dignity isn't a spreadsheet trick. It's a story you tell yourself, and it has to be true in both directions. The story says: "I don't need to impress you to be okay." And it also says: "I respect myself too much to accept a life that exhausts me." That story changes how you experience money. Purchases stop being announcements. Savings stop being punishment. You stop swinging between binge and purge, because you're no longer at war with yourself.

There's no universal threshold. Two people can spend the same amount with opposite results. One buys insulation and freedom, the other buys noise and upkeep. The difference is intention. Each time you buy something, ask: what story will this force me to live tomorrow? If it raises fixed costs, it narrows your choices. If it raises your capacity, it widens them. People love to believe that more income is the answer. The truth is the spread between income and lifestyle is the answer. That spread is shaped as much by standards as by salary.

Over time, the benefits outweigh the sacrifices. Your friends won't remember what you drove, but they'll remember you weren't desperate. Your children won't recall how fashionable your kitchen looked, but they'll remember your presence, unburdened by financial panic. Your future self won't thank you for years spent collecting approval—it will thank you for the space you created to think and the pride you never mortgaged.

If the first rule—save before you spend—sets the sequence, this one sets the tone. You can only save first for decades if the life that follows feels livable. When you live below your means but above your dignity, wealth is no stunt. It becomes a rhythm you can sustain. And rhythm is what turns arithmetic into a life.

## Rule 3 – Compounding is invisible until it manifests

The human brain struggles with exponential growth. We think in straight lines, imagining tomorrow as today plus a little more. Compounding mocks that instinct. It grows quietly, almost invisibly, and for years looks unimpressive. Then, seemingly overnight, it erupts into something that feels like magic. But there's no magic here–only arithmetic and time, guarded by patience.

Take Warren Buffett. Over ninety percent of his fortune came after his sixtieth birthday. Not because he suddenly became smarter, but because compounding finally had enough runway to reveal its force. The same logic applies to everyone, just at different scales. In the beginning, saving and investing feel pointless. The returns are pennies, the growth microscopic. Most people give up here. They ditch the plan, chase the next trend, and in doing so restart the clock. What they don't see is that compounding asks for one thing only: uninterrupted time.

That invisibility is its test. Compounding demands you keep going without proof. You have to endure the boredom of small results, the jeers from those chasing excitement, and the nagging voice telling you the numbers aren't moving. The challenge isn't mathematical–it's emotional. Markets reward the ones who can wait, not the ones who calculate the fastest.

And then, without warning, the flat line bends. The graph that looked lifeless suddenly arcs upward. What was small becomes meaningful; what was meaningful becomes extraordinary. The shift feels explosive, even though nothing about your behavior changed. You simply stayed in the game long enough for the invisible to become visible.

The tragedy is that most never reach this point. They underestimate how late the payoff arrives. They forget that time horizon is the most powerful variable in building wealth. Double the time and the results more than double. Stretch the horizon and compounding does work you could never replicate with sheer effort.

Compounding isn't limited to money. Reputation grows when kindness compounds. Knowledge grows when learning compounds. Habits compound into identity. Each builds quietly, so slowly it feels like nothing is happening–until one day you look around and see results that others call luck. What they didn't see was the long stretch of monotony you endured.

The rule here isn't simply "let it grow." It's "don't interrupt it." Every withdrawal, every panic sale, every lifestyle upgrade that forces you to cash out–these are compounding's enemies. The engine is fragile. Protect it from your impatience. Compounding isn't a sprint. It's a slow drip that becomes a flood, but only for those willing to stay when it still looks like a trickle.

## Rule 4 – Own assets, not just income

Income feels powerful. It lands regularly, it makes you feel capable, it convinces you that you are secure. But income is fragile. It stops the moment you do. Assets are different. They keep working when you don't. They produce value when you sleep, when you are sick, even when you are gone. That is why the difference between income and assets explains why some high earners end up with nothing, while others with modest salaries retire free.

Most people mistake income for wealth because income is visible. A paycheck feels real in a way that a portfolio doesn't. But the danger is simple: income is a stream tied to your labor. If labor stops, the stream dries up. An asset is a reservoir. It collects and produces independent of your direct effort. Stocks, real estate, businesses, intellectual property—all are assets because they generate flows beyond your hours.

The trap of income is lifestyle creep. The more you earn, the more you spend. The new salary funds the new house, the new car, the new vacations. Expenses rise to match income, and the treadmill accelerates. Assets, on the other hand, break the treadmill. They separate survival from your body's ability to grind. Once your assets produce enough to cover your needs, income becomes optional. That is the inflection point where freedom begins.

Owning assets is not about being fancy or chasing complexity. It is about asking, for every dollar you control: will this dollar vanish the moment I stop working, or will it keep producing without me? If the answer is the first, you are renting a lifestyle. If the answer is the second, you are building wealth.

The subtlety is that not all assets are equal. Some produce cash flow consistently; others rely on appreciation that may or may not arrive. Some are liquid; others are locked away. The point is not to find the perfect one, but to own enough of them that your life is not chained entirely to your own labor. The shift from income to assets is the shift from fragile to durable.

In the long run, people remember how you lived, not how much you earned. Income pays for today. Assets write the story of tomorrow. You cannot retire on a memory of high paychecks. You can only retire on what those paychecks built.

## Rule 5 – Invest in what you understand

The financial world thrives on mystery. Acronyms multiply, products are dressed in complex structures, and every cycle produces a new vehicle promising returns that ordinary people "just don't get." That obscurity is not an accident. It sells. Complexity creates the illusion of sophistication, and people assume that the more complicated something sounds, the more profitable it must be. But wealth is rarely the prize of those who chase what they don't understand. It belongs to those who admit their circle of competence and stay inside it.

Understanding is not about predicting the future. Nobody knows where interest rates will be in five years or which company will dominate technology in twenty. Understanding means knowing how an asset creates value, how it can fail, and what assumptions it relies on. If you cannot explain to a child how the thing you own actually works, you don't own an asset–you own a bet you don't comprehend. And bets you don't comprehend tend to pay out only for the people who sold them to you.

The great risk of investing outside your understanding is that you will not know when you are wrong. A bad investment inside your circle of competence teaches you something you can use. A bad investment outside it only leaves you poorer and confused. Wealth compounds when lessons compound, and lessons require comprehension.

This rule is not a call to be timid. It is a call to be deliberate. You can and should stretch the edges of your knowledge. Read, ask, study. But buy only when you can articulate in plain words what you're buying, why it's valuable, what could kill it, and how you'll know if that's happening. Complexity will always tempt you. The crowd will always chase the next obscure miracle. Your advantage is not being smarter than them—it is being clear when they are noisy.

Fortunes collapse when people surrender understanding for excitement. Fortunes endure when people remember that clarity outperforms cleverness. Invest in what you understand, because in a crisis, the only conviction that keeps you steady is the conviction you can explain to yourself without notes.

## Rule 6 – Diversify, but don't dilute

Diversification is one of the oldest rules in finance, and also one of the most misunderstood. At its core, diversification is survival. It is a shield against the randomness of life. No matter how confident you are, the world is bigger than your models. Businesses fail. Markets collapse. Governments change the rules mid-game. Diversification says: I will not let one accident erase me.

But like all shields, diversification can be misused. Too little, and one blow destroys you. Too much, and the shield is so heavy you can't move forward. Real diversification is not about owning everything. It is about balancing enough exposure to reduce fragility without spreading yourself so thin that no success matters.

Think of it this way: concentration builds wealth; diversification preserves it. You need both, but not in equal measure at every stage. The young entrepreneur pours effort into one venture because survival requires focus. The family office spreads across industries and regions because survival now requires resilience. Dilution happens when you forget which stage you are in and scatter resources so widely that victory in any one area cannot change your life.

Indexes exist for a reason: they provide broad resilience when you cannot or do not want to pick winners. But if you treat every opportunity like another line item in a museum of investments, you are no longer diversified–you are paralyzed. The wealthy often hold fewer bets than the average investor, but they understand those bets deeply, and they balance them with ballast that keeps failure from being fatal.

The lesson is not complicated, but it is uncomfortable. Diversification means admitting ignorance: you don't know the future, so you hedge against it. Avoiding dilution means admitting limits: you can't own everything, so you concentrate where you have conviction. The art is in holding those admissions at the same time.

Diversify enough to survive. Concentrate enough to matter. Anything else is either gambling with your future or burying it in assets that will never change your life.

## Rule 7 – Cash flow is king

Wealth is often described in terms of net worth. People like to measure themselves by the size of the number on their balance sheet. But net worth is an illusion if it cannot pay the bills. Assets can be inflated, valuations can be misleading, markets can assign temporary prices that flatter or humiliate you. None of that matters if you cannot produce steady cash flow.

Cash flow is what keeps the lights on. It is the bloodstream of every business and every household. A portfolio that looks enormous on paper but produces no liquidity is like owning a desert full of oil without the means to drill. You might technically be rich, but practically you are fragile.

The dot-com bubble produced plenty of paper billionaires. When the bubble burst, what mattered wasn't how big their market cap had been—it was how much actual cash their businesses generated. Many had none, so they vanished overnight. The same story repeats every generation: illusions of wealth collapse into dust when cash flow proves absent.

Cash flow matters because it creates endurance. It allows you to survive downturns without selling assets at fire-sale prices. It funds opportunities when others are too constrained to act. It buys patience in markets that punish impatience. With cash flow, you can wait. Without it, you are forced to react. Wealth is less about what you own than about how long you can last without panic.

Even in personal finance, the lesson holds. Two families can both have a net worth of a million dollars. One holds it all in a primary residence and retirement accounts they cannot touch without penalty. The other holds a mix of cash, bonds, and dividend-paying stocks. Both are technically millionaires. Only one can cover six months of bills without disruption. The other is wealthy only on paper.

Cash flow also teaches humility. It forces you to ask hard questions: how much of this wealth can I actually use, today, without destroying tomorrow? How much is tied up in assets that depend on the kindness of markets? When your wealth only exists if someone else agrees to buy from you at the right price, you are not independent–you are negotiating with strangers.

The paradox is that strong cash flow rarely looks glamorous. It is boring businesses, steady dividends, repetitive rents, subscriptions quietly charged every month. The real engines of wealth are not the headlines. They are the drips and streams that keep flowing long after the excitement fades. Cash flow doesn't make you famous. It makes you free.

## Rule 8 – Turn skills into capital

Every skill you have can take two paths. You can sell it for income, or you can transform it into capital. The difference is subtle but life-changing.

A doctor who sees patients is trading skill for income. A doctor who builds a clinic, hires other doctors, and owns the infrastructure is turning skill into capital. A writer who freelances for magazines earns income. A writer who owns rights to books that keep selling has turned words into capital.

The danger of relying only on income is that it dies the moment you stop showing up. Income is fragile because it demands your presence. Capital is resilient because it scales beyond your hours. Transforming skills into capital is how you stop working for money and make money start working for you.

This is not easy. Turning skills into capital requires delay. Instead of taking the highest-paying gig today, you invest time in building something that might not pay for months or years. That sacrifice feels unbearable in the moment, especially when peers flaunt faster earnings. But the payoff is asymmetric. A skill sold for income is gone forever once the hour is worked. A skill turned into capital continues producing without your presence, sometimes long after you've moved on.

The wealthiest people are not always the most talented. They are often the ones who figured out how to capture their talent in a structure that outlives their effort. They learned to package skills into products, services, businesses, intellectual property–anything that multiplies reach without multiplying hours. That multiplier is capital.

There's also a psychological reward. Income buys comfort, but capital buys calm. Knowing that your skills have been bottled into a structure that keeps paying even when you rest transforms how you experience risk. You no longer fear a dry spell, because your capital keeps dripping in the background. That drip is dignity.

The hardest part is patience. Early in your career, income feels like survival and capital feels like fantasy. But every fortune is built by someone who paused the chase for today's highest rate and asked: how can I build something that pays me tomorrow even if I do nothing? That question is the hinge between working for a living and living off what you built.

Skills are seeds. You can eat them now for quick nourishment, or you can plant them as capital and harvest for a lifetime. One choice makes you busy forever. The other makes you free.

## Rule 9 – Build multiple income streams

Depending on a single source of income is like balancing your entire life on one leg. It may hold for a while, maybe even for years, but eventually, pressure comes from somewhere you didn't predict, and the structure collapses. Jobs disappear, industries fade, health breaks, companies fail. When your whole survival depends on a single stream, fragility is your default condition.

The idea of multiple income streams is not about greed. It is about resilience. Each stream you add to your life—dividends, rental income, royalties, side businesses, consulting, digital products—becomes another leg under the table. One leg wobbling doesn't topple the whole. This is not just theory. History is full of fortunes that survived downturns because the owners had something else paying them when one source dried up.

The trap most people fall into is binary thinking. They either stick with one job, or they scatter themselves across ten half-baked ventures that exhaust them. The point is not quantity for its own sake. It is diversity with weight. A second stream that contributes ten percent of your needs might be the difference between panic and patience in a downturn. A third stream might not make you rich, but it may stop you from selling an asset you love at the worst possible moment.

Multiple income streams also change psychology. When you are chained to one source, you negotiate from weakness. You need the job, the client, the contract, which means they have leverage over you. When you have other inflows, you negotiate from calm. You can walk away. Options create confidence, and confidence creates better outcomes. It is not just the money. It is the posture the money allows.

The irony is that building additional streams usually starts small—so small it feels like a distraction. A blog that earns fifty dollars a month, a tiny online store, a spare room rented occasionally. People dismiss these because they don't move the needle today. What they miss is the asymmetry. Small streams can grow. Some stay modest, but others compound into independence. The wealthy rarely knew in advance which stream would become dominant. They just kept planting.

The rule is simple: if one stream dries up, you want to keep breathing. You don't need dozens of rivers. You need enough trickles that the drought of one does not define your future. Multiple income streams are not about being everywhere. They are about never being cornered.

## Rule 10 – Leverage technology, not just labor

For most of history, wealth was a function of labor. More hours, more output. The body was the limit, and the day had only so many hours. Technology shattered that equation. It created tools that multiply effort far beyond the capacity of one human body. The printing press multiplied words. The assembly line multiplied hands. Software multiplies ideas. The internet multiplies reach. Technology is labor's most powerful ally because it detaches output from hours.

Leverage is what separates those who merely work hard from those who see their effort scale. A teacher who gives a lecture earns once. A teacher who records that lecture and distributes it online earns indefinitely. A shopkeeper who sells in one town caps his reach. A shopkeeper who builds an online store has no cap at all. In each case, the same skill, the same product, is multiplied by a tool. The wealth difference between those who adopt leverage and those who don't is staggering.

Labor is linear; technology is exponential. This is why some fortunes look unexplainable. They are not built on superior intelligence alone. They are built on the compounding power of leverage. A coder is not necessarily smarter than a carpenter, but the coder's work can be replicated a million times at near-zero cost. The carpenter's cannot. Technology is the multiplier, not the intelligence gap.

But there is a trap. Technology is not a substitute for value. Automating nonsense only scales nonsense. Multiplying a bad idea only destroys faster. The foundation must be a skill, a product, or a service that actually creates value. Once you have that, technology amplifies it. Without that, technology exposes weakness.

This rule is not about chasing every new tool. It is about asking: what in my work can be replicated, distributed, automated, or scaled beyond my direct effort? What process repeats often enough that a machine could handle it? What product is valuable enough that thousands of people would pay for it if only they could access it? Technology answers these questions.

The irony is that many people resist leverage because they believe it threatens authenticity. They equate hand-crafted attention with virtue. But history shows the opposite: the people who leverage technology wisely often create more time for authenticity. They automate the repetitive so they can focus on the meaningful. Technology does not replace you. It liberates you.

Wealth built purely on labor ends the moment the labor stops. Wealth built with technology endures, because the machine keeps humming long after you've gone home. The question is not whether you should leverage technology. The question is whether you are willing to keep trading hours for outcomes while others trade hours for multipliers.

## Rule 11 – Use debt sparingly—and only as leverage, never as lifestyle

Debt is one of the most misunderstood forces in finance. For some, it feels like opportunity—the chance to buy what you want now and figure it out later. For others, it feels like poison, a trap that enslaves those who touch it. The truth lives between those extremes. Debt is not inherently evil. But it is dangerous, because it is one of the few financial tools that magnifies both your best and your worst decisions.

The difference comes down to purpose. Lifestyle debt is a promise your future self makes to clean up the mess your present self is creating. It buys houses that are too big, cars that are too fast, and luxuries that fade the moment they're unboxed. Leverage, on the other hand, is debt tied to productive assets—assets that generate cash flow strong enough to service the debt and leave something left over. The first version makes you fragile. The second can make you strong.

The key is survival under stress. A business with prudent leverage can weather a downturn because the underlying cash flows don't vanish with a bad quarter. A household with lifestyle debt collapses the moment income wobbles. One is a calculated risk with redundancy built in. The other is a house of cards that depends on perfection.

The hardest part is that lifestyle debt often disguises itself as leverage. People tell themselves their car is an "investment" because it lets them get to work. Their vacation is "networking." Their oversized house is "equity." These justifications collapse under scrutiny. If the thing you financed does not create income or appreciate in durable value, it is consumption on credit. And consumption on credit is not wealth. It is servitude.

Another danger is timing. Debt lives in the tails of probability. It doesn't ruin you when everything is average. It ruins you when multiple bad things happen at once—when income drops, expenses rise, interest rates adjust, and refinancing isn't available. These moments don't arrive often, but they arrive eventually. You cannot build a strategy on the assumption that they won't.

The irony is that the people who use debt best are the ones least dependent on it. They already have assets, cash flow, and margin of safety. Debt is a tool they deploy sparingly to accelerate a structure that would survive without it. Those who need debt the most—because they have no cushion—are the ones least able to withstand it.

The rule is simple but harsh: never use debt to live bigger than your future can afford. Use it, if you must, to own productive assets that pay for themselves even under pressure. And even then, treat debt like fire. Contained, it cooks your food. Uncontained, it burns down your house.

## Rule 12 – Learn to read balance sheets

Numbers don't lie, but they often whisper. The balance sheet is the quietest of all financial statements. It doesn't shout about profits like the income statement. It doesn't dramatize movement like the cash flow statement. It sits still, showing what is owned, what is owed, and what is left. Yet within that stillness lies the truth about resilience.

Assets, liabilities, equity. Three categories that answer one essential question: how fragile is this entity, and what would it take to break it? A business with a billion in assets and nine hundred million in liabilities looks big, but it is one mistake away from insolvency. A family with a modest home and no debt looks small, but they are built to endure. The balance sheet reveals not size, but margin. And margin is survival.

Assets deserve scrutiny. Cash is simple. Everything else is a claim disguised as certainty. Accounts receivable are promises. Inventory is a bet that what you hold today will be wanted tomorrow. Property is valuable until you need to sell it fast, and then it is only worth what someone will pay under stress. The balance sheet forces you to ask: what here would still be money in my pocket if the world panicked tomorrow?

Liabilities are less subtle. They are contracts with teeth. The number matters, but the terms matter more. Fixed versus floating rates, short versus long maturities, secured versus unsecured—all change the story. A company can appear stable until its debt rolls over at higher rates, and suddenly what was manageable becomes impossible.

Individuals face the same risk when they stack short-term obligations against long-term uncertainty.

Equity is the buffer, but also the confession. Thin equity means owners have left little room for error. Thick equity means the same shocks can be absorbed without collapse. But even equity requires honesty. If it's built on inflated valuations, it's optimism, not cushion.

The lesson is not academic. Every financial crisis, every corporate collapse, every household bankruptcy has been visible first on the balance sheet. It's where optimism hides and fragility accumulates. When the music stops, the income statement can't save you. The balance sheet has already decided your fate.

Individuals need this skill as much as investors. Most people only track income and expenses, but without a personal balance sheet they miss the bigger picture. How much of what you own produces cash versus demanding it? How much of your net worth is liquid versus locked away? Are your obligations fixed while your income is variable? The answers decide not whether you are wealthy today, but whether you will stay wealthy tomorrow.

To read balance sheets is to develop skepticism, and skepticism is a shield. You stop believing growth stories that require perfect conditions. You stop envying people with swollen assets that collapse under stress. You start preferring boring resilience over exciting fragility. That preference alone can save a fortune.

The paradox is that strong balance sheets often look unimpressive. They hoard cash, avoid leverage, and sacrifice efficiency.

They are mocked in boom times for being too conservative. But when the cycle turns, they are the ones left standing. Strength often looks wasteful until waste is the only thing that breaks.

Learn to read balance sheets, because in the end, they don't just reveal numbers. They reveal character—the willingness to forgo appearances in favor of endurance. And endurance is what wealth really is: the ability to stay in the game long enough for compounding to work in your favor.

# Rule 13 – Taxes are the biggest hidden expense

Most people think of taxes only once a year–when the forms are due and the accountant sends the bill. But taxes are not an event. They are a shadow that follows every financial move you make. They are the quiet partner in every deal, the invisible cost embedded in almost every paycheck, sale, and transfer. And because they are hidden in plain sight, people underestimate their power.

Consider this: two investors earn the same return over thirty years. One ignores taxes, letting them eat away at gains every year. The other structures wisely–using tax-deferred accounts, timing sales, harvesting losses, choosing vehicles that minimize friction. The second ends up with double the wealth of the first, without earning a higher return. The difference wasn't intelligence. It was awareness of the largest silent expense in finance.

Taxes compound in reverse. Every dollar you lose to the taxman is not just gone today; it's gone forever from the compounding engine. A tax paid on a gain today is also the lost growth that gain would have produced for decades. That is why seemingly small differences in tax treatment create enormous gulfs over time. The math is simple. The psychology is harder.

Most people chase headline returns and ignore after-tax returns. They compare stocks, funds, or properties without asking what portion of the gain they actually keep. It is like bragging about a high salary without admitting that most of it is consumed by rent and debt.

Wealth is not about what you make. It is about what you keep after everyone else takes their cut.

Avoiding taxes entirely is a fantasy—and often illegal. But minimizing them is not just legal, it is essential. Smart investors don't evade. They optimize. They defer when possible, align assets with tax treatment, and remember that turnover is expensive. They accept that sometimes the best move is not to do something, because every action has a hidden partner demanding a share.

The government will always get paid. The question is whether you design your financial life in a way that leaves room for compounding to work on your behalf instead of theirs. Taxes are the single largest controllable expense for many wealthy individuals. Ignore them, and you will work for others. Respect them, and you will keep more of what compounding owes you.

## Rule 14 – Automate savings and investments

Discipline is fragile. It wavers with mood, weakens under stress, collapses when temptation whispers. Automation is discipline without the burden of willpower. It takes the best version of your intentions and locks them into a system that keeps working on the days you would rather quit.

The biggest obstacle to saving is not ability; it is behavior. Most people know they should save more. They fail because saving requires a conscious choice every time, and conscious choices are vulnerable to excuses. "This month is special." "I'll start after the holiday." "Next raise, I'll get serious." Life produces endless reasons not to save. Automation eliminates the question altogether. When money moves straight from income into savings or investments without asking your permission, there is nothing to debate. The decision was made once and made permanent.

Automation works because it aligns with human weakness instead of fighting it. You don't need to be disciplined every month. You only need to be disciplined once: when you set the system up. After that, inertia becomes your ally. The same psychological bias that keeps people trapped in bad habits now keeps you trapped in good ones.

This principle is why retirement accounts work. Left to voluntary contributions, most people would save far too little. With automatic deductions, they save without thinking, and decades later the totals look miraculous. It is also why subscription models are so profitable for companies: once the payment is automated, people rarely cancel. The same force that makes subscriptions dangerous can make your financial future secure.

The beauty of automation is that it protects you from yourself during extremes. In bull markets, when greed whispers that you should buy more, your system keeps you steady. In bear markets, when fear screams to sell, your system continues to buy because it doesn't have emotions. Automated behavior is boring, and boring is the point.

There will always be people who prefer to keep everything manual, convinced they can out-discipline their impulses. A few succeed. Most don't. The difference between those who build wealth and those who don't is rarely intelligence. It is consistency. Automation guarantees consistency in a way nothing else can.

If saving first is the foundation of wealth, automating saving is the insurance that the foundation won't crack. It transforms a good intention into a lifelong habit. And over decades, the quiet drip of automated contributions becomes an ocean.

## Rule 15 – Negotiate everything

Most people think negotiation belongs only in boardrooms and contract signings. In reality, negotiation is everywhere. Prices are suggestions, salaries are starting points, terms are proposals, and policies are drafts. The people who quietly accumulate wealth are often those who treat negotiation as a way of life, not as a rare event.

Negotiation does not mean conflict. It means refusing to accept that the first number you are given must also be the last. It means recognizing that most financial interactions are shaped by incentives, and incentives leave room for movement. Landlords want occupancy. Employers want retention. Vendors want recurring business. Banks want relationships. Each of these desires is leverage for you, if you learn to see it.

The tragedy is that most people never ask. They are afraid of offending, or they assume that prices are immovable. They leave wealth on the table because silence feels safer than the possibility of rejection. But rejection costs nothing. Silence costs everything. A five percent discount negotiated on every meaningful transaction over a lifetime adds up to more than most people's investment returns. A slightly better salary or interest rate compounds into freedom that looks invisible at first but becomes undeniable over decades.

The art of negotiation is not aggression but preparation. You win before you ask by understanding what the other side values. If you can make them feel they're winning, they will happily give you more than you expected. The wealthiest negotiators are not the loudest. They are the most curious. They ask what matters to the other party, and they design agreements that satisfy both sides.

Negotiating everything also changes your psychology. It builds confidence, not because you always win, but because you learn to stop assuming power is elsewhere. The simple act of asking rebalances the relationship. You stop living as a passive consumer of terms and start living as a co-author. That identity shift compounds across a lifetime in ways no spreadsheet can capture.

The lesson is clear: wealth does not only come from earning more or investing better. It also comes from refusing to accept the first offer. The world belongs to those who ask.

## Rule 16 – Insurance is protection, not investment

Insurance is one of the most misunderstood financial tools. Many people see it as a waste of money because they rarely "use" it. Others see it as a clever investment vehicle, convinced that some policies can replace stocks or real estate. Both views miss the truth. Insurance is not meant to make you rich. It is meant to prevent you from being ruined.

The purpose of insurance is survival. It exists to protect against events so catastrophic that they could erase decades of progress. You don't buy health insurance because you expect to get sick tomorrow. You buy it because a single illness without coverage can bankrupt you. You don't buy life insurance because you think you're about to die. You buy it because your family's survival shouldn't depend on your ability to predict the future.

The mistake people make is treating insurance as an "investment." Salespeople encourage this by pitching whole-life policies or elaborate hybrids that promise returns alongside protection. But the returns are usually mediocre, the fees high, and the liquidity poor. Insurance should be judged by the quality of its protection, not by its yield. When you try to make insurance carry the burden of investing, you weaken both.

There is also a behavioral misunderstanding. People resent paying premiums because they hope never to use the product. They feel cheated if a year goes by with no claim. But this is backwards. The best outcome is that your insurance feels like a waste, because it means disaster never came. Insurance is one of the few products you buy hoping never to need. Its value lies in the absence of crisis.

The wealthy understand this. They insure aggressively against tail risks that could end their journey, but they don't over-insure against minor inconveniences. They carry high deductibles for small losses they can afford, and they protect ruthlessly against losses they cannot. They see insurance not as a way to get richer, but as a way to guarantee they stay in the game long enough for compounding to make them richer.

The rule is simple: never confuse insurance with investment. One is about growth, the other about survival. And survival always comes first.

# Rule 17 – Protect downside before chasing upside

The world worships upside. We celebrate returns, growth, jackpots, and lucky breaks. Yet wealth that lasts is rarely about how high you climb. It is about how far you fall when gravity shows up. Protecting the downside is not glamorous, but it is the foundation that allows you to stay in the game long enough to enjoy the upside when it finally arrives.

Every financial history is filled with cycles. Booms and busts, bull markets and bear markets, promotions and layoffs. Nobody escapes the rhythm. The mistake most people make is assuming they can skip the busts. They build fragile structures designed only for good weather, and then act surprised when storms arrive. Protecting the downside is admitting the storms are inevitable.

What does this look like in practice? It means keeping cash reserves even when interest rates make them look pointless. It means diversifying across industries and geographies even when concentration seems more profitable. It means refusing leverage that looks smart in bull markets but suicidal in recessions. It means saying no to opportunities you don't fully understand, because ignorance is not protection.

The psychology here is crucial. Protecting downside feels boring in the moment. It feels like holding back. It feels like being overly cautious. But wealth is not a sprint. It is a survival game. The person who endures the longest wins, because compounding rewards the last player standing. Upside compounds only if you are around to let it.

There is a paradox worth remembering: protecting downside often feels inefficient. You carry cash that earns little. You diversify into assets that don't soar. You turn down leverage that could make your returns explode. But inefficiency in the short term is resilience in the long term. A system that looks "optimized" for maximum gain is usually optimized for maximum fragility. Fragility is not wealth. Endurance is.

Protecting downside before chasing upside is not about pessimism. It is about humility. It is about recognizing that you don't need to catch every wave, but you cannot afford to sink with one bad storm. Protect the downside, and the upside will take care of itself.

# Rule 18 – Build assets that pay while you sleep

Time is the one resource nobody can expand. You can work harder, smarter, longer–but eventually the day ends, and your body insists on rest. Wealth is built by those who find a way to make money flow even when they are not awake to supervise it.

Assets that pay while you sleep are the holy grail of financial independence. Rental properties, dividend-paying stocks, royalties from intellectual property, automated businesses, digital products, software–anything that continues generating cash without your direct presence. The wealthy are not just workers with high incomes. They are owners of machines that keep humming when they step away.

The beauty of sleep-paying assets is not only in the money. It is in the psychology. When you know that income arrives even when you rest, you stop fearing every disruption. You can take time off, change careers, or endure downturns without the panic that grips those who depend entirely on their waking hours. The paycheck stops the moment you stop showing up. The asset doesn't. That difference is freedom.

But building these assets requires delay. They rarely appear overnight. Writing a book that pays royalties takes months of work with no guarantee of success. Building a business system that operates without you demands sacrifice and reinvestment. Buying dividend stocks means forgoing consumption today. The upfront effort feels unfairly large compared to the slow trickle that follows. And yet, the trickle compounds. A dollar that arrives while you sleep feels smaller than a salary dollar, but it carries magic: it arrives without effort. Over time, those dollars accumulate into rivers.

There is also a dignity in this kind of wealth. It breaks the chain between effort and survival. It turns money into a servant, not a master. It lets you align your waking hours with purpose instead of obligation. You are no longer renting your time. You are renting your structures, your ideas, your ownership.

The danger is confusing speculation with sleep-paying assets. A stock that might rise in value is not the same as one that regularly distributes dividends. A property that "should" appreciate is not the same as one with steady tenants. Assets that pay while you sleep are not about fantasy—they are about reliable flows. Dreaming of price charts is not the same as designing systems that cash flow.

At some point, everyone grows tired. Everyone wants to stop working for survival and start working for meaning. Those who built assets that pay while they sleep have that option. Those who didn't must keep running. In the end, wealth is not just about how much you make awake. It is about what keeps arriving while you rest.

## Rule 19 – Keep liquidity for crises and opportunities

Liquidity is boring until the day you need it. On paper, an illiquid fortune can look impressive–properties, private businesses, restricted stock. But the moment a crisis arrives, those numbers become fragile. You cannot sell half a building to pay the hospital bill. You cannot mortgage goodwill to cover payroll when banks are nervous. Liquidity is not the flashiest part of wealth, but it is the part that decides whether you survive shocks or collapse under them.

The paradox of liquidity is that it always feels excessive right up until it feels insufficient. Carrying cash looks like weakness in bull markets. People will tell you it's lazy money, that inflation is eating it, that you're missing out on gains. And they are right–until they're not. Because when the tide goes out, liquidity buys you time, and time buys you everything. It buys patience, bargaining power, and the ability to say no to desperate deals. It turns you into the calm buyer in a panic-driven market.

Liquidity is not just for crises. It is for opportunities. Almost every great fortune has a story of someone who had cash when nobody else did. Recessions, sell-offs, sudden dislocations–these are not only dangers, they are invitations. But the invitation is extended only to those who have liquidity. Without it, you watch opportunity pass by while you scramble to cover survival.

There is also a psychological dimension. Liquidity reduces anxiety. Knowing you can cover months or years of expenses changes how you make decisions. You stop thinking in terms of desperation and start thinking in terms of choice. The wealthy value liquidity not because it maximizes return, but because it maximizes freedom.

Liquidity is like oxygen. When it is abundant, you don't notice. When it is scarce, it is all you can think about. The rule is simple: carry more liquidity than you think you need. You will not regret it when the storm comes—or when the bargain of a lifetime arrives at your door.

## Rule 20 – A small win repeated beats a windfall wasted

The world loves windfalls. Lottery winners, overnight IPO millionaires, athletes with giant contracts–these stories capture imagination. But the data is cruel. Most who receive sudden wealth lose it quickly. The reason is simple: without habits, money is a guest, not a resident. A fortune dropped into your lap without rhythm to hold it will vanish as quickly as it came.

Wealth that lasts is rarely built in explosions. It is built in increments. A small win, repeated, compounds into something astonishing over time. Saving a little each month, closing steady contracts, reinvesting modest dividends–these look trivial in the moment, but they are the bricks of permanence. Windfalls create headlines. Small wins create legacies.

The psychology is what matters most. When you rely on windfalls, you live in hope and spectacle. You chase jackpots, trade recklessly, and assume the future will look like the best version of the past. When you rely on small wins, you live in discipline and patience. You stop needing miracles, because you built a system that doesn't depend on them.

The danger of windfalls is not only the lack of habit. It is the pressure they create. Sudden wealth invites sudden expectations. Friends, family, and even strangers treat you differently. You feel compelled to upgrade lifestyle to match the new number, but the upgrades become recurring costs. What felt like abundance quickly turns into strain. Without the rhythm of small wins to defend it, the windfall becomes a trap.

History rewards those who understood that repetition beats explosion. The investor who reinvests dividends for forty years ends with more than the speculator who doubled their money twice and lost it all on the third attempt. The entrepreneur who builds a business that grows ten percent every year is wealthier in the end than the one who tries to multiply by ten overnight and burns out.

The rule is not to reject windfalls. If fortune smiles, accept it. But never rely on it. Build habits so strong that even if the windfall never comes, you are still free. A small win repeated is not exciting to watch. But it is thrilling to live, because one day you wake up and realize the life you wanted was built not by miracles, but by rhythm.

## Rule 20 – A small win repeated beats a windfall wasted

Most people overestimate the power of sudden fortune and underestimate the quiet force of repetition. The world is fascinated by jackpots–lottery winners, overnight millionaires, tech founders who strike gold. These stories feel magnetic because they compress success into a single dramatic moment. But what the headlines rarely show is how often these windfalls are wasted. The money comes in a flood and leaves just as quickly, because the recipient never built the habits to hold it.

Wealth is not about how much you get in one stroke. It is about how you behave repeatedly when the world is not watching. A small win–a habit of saving a little, investing modestly, or steadily improving a skill–feels insignificant in the short term. Yet when you stack thousands of these small wins, the result dwarfs most windfalls. Compounding needs rhythm, not drama.

The danger of windfalls is psychological. Easy money teaches reckless lessons. You start to believe money is plentiful, replaceable, and always within reach. That belief encourages bad bets and careless spending. Small wins teach the opposite. They teach patience, discipline, and respect for the process. They build identity. You stop being someone who "got lucky once" and become someone who "does the right thing every day."

And that identity is why small wins survive where windfalls collapse. The person who earns slowly develops systems–budgets, guardrails, values–that keep wealth intact. The person who wins suddenly has none of these defenses. They go from zero to excess without the immune system of habit, and the money leaves as quickly as it arrived.

The truth is that small wins feel dull. They don't impress your friends or make headlines. But boredom is the real secret to wealth. If you can endure it, you will wake up one day surrounded by results that outsiders will call luck. You will know it was rhythm. A small win repeated is not glamorous, but it is undefeated.

## Rule 21 – Wealth is not money

Money and wealth are cousins, not twins. Money is a number on a statement. Wealth is the ability to endure, to choose, to say no. You can have money without wealth–just ask the highly paid executive who drowns in debt, the celebrity who files for bankruptcy, or the investor with paper gains who has no liquidity when crisis hits. Wealth is not the number you show others. It is the condition you live with when the world turns against you.

Money measures transactions. Wealth measures time. If you can cover your needs without selling your soul, you are wealthy even if the number looks modest. If you cannot walk away from a toxic client, an exhausting job, or a fragile structure, you may have money but you are not wealthy.

The confusion comes from visibility. Money is easy to show–cars, houses, vacations. Wealth is invisible–calm, security, freedom. You cannot always see it from the outside. In fact, the people who look the richest are often the ones who traded true wealth for appearances. They spent the freedom they hadn't yet earned to broadcast success.

The wealthy are not always who you think. They may drive ordinary cars, live in modest houses, and avoid displays. What they have is control over their time, confidence in their resilience, and the quiet power to choose. They don't need to prove wealth because they feel it every day in their ability to endure.

Money is what you count. Wealth is what you experience. One can vanish in a transaction. The other survives crises, downturns, and even death, because it lives in reputation, relationships, and systems. That is why the first foundation of lasting prosperity is remembering this: money is a tool, not the destination. Wealth is the condition of freedom that the tool makes possible.

## Rule 22 – Enough is a moving target

The most dangerous word in finance is "more." It sounds harmless–who doesn't want more security, more comfort, more opportunity? But "more" has no finish line. The moment you reach one milestone, another appears just beyond it. A higher salary, a bigger house, a nicer car, a larger fund. What once felt like abundance now feels like baseline, and you start running again. Enough keeps moving, because the human mind is wired for comparison.

This moving target is why many people earn more than they ever dreamed of yet still feel poor. They are not measuring against their needs. They are measuring against their neighbor's new kitchen, their colleague's promotion, or a billionaire's net worth splashed across the news. Comparison is a thief that robs every victory of its satisfaction.

The tragedy is that if you never define enough, you can never win. You will always live in a state of almost–almost secure, almost satisfied, almost there. And "almost" is the most exhausting place to live. It is a treadmill that runs faster as you go, leaving you breathless but never closer to arrival.

Enough is not about mediocrity. It is about sovereignty. It is the ability to say: "Beyond this point, the cost of more outweighs the benefit." Enough is a line you draw for yourself, not for others. It might be the ability to cover emergencies, to retire without fear, to spend freely on experiences that matter, to provide stability for your family. What matters is that it is yours.

The wealthiest people are not those who never want more. They are those who know when to stop wanting. Enough is a declaration of independence from the moving target of envy. Without it, you are rich in numbers but poor in peace. With it, you may not have the largest fortune, but you will have the rarest one: contentment.

## Rule 23 – Freedom is the ultimate currency

Strip away the symbols of wealth–houses, cars, accounts, titles–and ask what people actually want. The answer, if they are honest, is freedom. Freedom to spend time as they wish, to choose work instead of needing it, to walk away from toxic people, to say no without fear. Money matters only because it buys this freedom. Without it, money is just paper.

Every financial decision can be measured against this question: does it increase or reduce my freedom? A high-paying job that chains you to misery may look impressive, but it is not wealth if you cannot leave. A modest portfolio that covers your needs without stress is more powerful than a fortune that owns you. Wealth is not measured by what you can buy. It is measured by what you can walk away from.

Freedom also compounds. The first taste–covering an emergency without debt–feels small but intoxicating. The next stage–turning down a bad client, taking a break without panic–expands it further. Over time, freedom becomes the true dividend of wise financial choices. The assets may be numbers in an account, but the reward is lived in hours, days, and decisions unshackled from necessity.

The paradox is that freedom rarely looks glamorous. It looks like a calendar without forced appointments. It looks like sleep without anxiety. It looks like being able to spend time with people you actually want to see. To outsiders, that may not look like wealth. But to the person living it, it is priceless.

Freedom is the ultimate currency because it buys the one thing money itself cannot: time that is truly yours. Lose that, and no fortune can replace it. Gain it, and even modest wealth feels like abundance.

## Rule 24 – Protect before you grow

Most people think wealth is built by chasing growth–higher returns, bigger risks, new ventures. But history shows that fortunes that endure are built first on protection. Before you grow, you must survive. Before you take on risk, you must have defenses in place. A castle without walls is just an invitation.

Protecting before you grow means asking hard questions: What can break me? What can force me to sell at the worst moment? What can erase years of progress overnight? The answers usually aren't complicated. Lack of liquidity. Excessive leverage. Overconcentration. Ignoring insurance. Underestimating taxes. These are the silent killers of compounding.

The psychology here is uncomfortable, because protection feels like wasted potential. Holding cash looks inefficient. Buying insurance feels like paying for nothing. Diversifying reduces upside in boom years. Yet all of these "inefficiencies" are what keep you alive long enough for compounding to reveal its power. Survival looks timid until the storm comes. Then it looks brilliant.

Consider two investors. One maximizes every dollar for growth, stretches leverage, and laughs at caution. The other grows slower, but carries reserves, insures against risks, and keeps concentration reasonable. For years, the first looks like a genius. Then a downturn arrives, and suddenly the castle without walls is rubble. The second survives, and survival is all compounding ever asks of you.

Protect before you grow is not a call for fear. It is a call for humility. Growth matters, but it is worthless if you cannot endure the setbacks that are guaranteed to arrive. You cannot enjoy the upside if you are already erased by the downside. First survive, then thrive. That sequence is not optional.

## Rule 25 – Reputation is capital

When people think of capital, they picture money, property, or equity. But one of the most powerful forms of capital is invisible: reputation. It cannot be printed, borrowed, or inherited easily. It must be earned, and once lost, it is almost impossible to restore.

Reputation is capital because it opens doors money cannot. A reputation for honesty earns trust, which lowers transaction costs. A reputation for reliability attracts opportunities others never even hear about. A reputation for discretion brings you into rooms where fortunes are decided quietly, long before the public sees the outcome. People often say "your network is your net worth," but what they mean is this: reputation is the currency that decides the size of your network.

The paradox is that reputation compounds slowly and can collapse instantly. You can spend decades building it through small, consistent actions–keeping promises, paying on time, treating people fairly–and lose it overnight with a single careless betrayal. Unlike money, there are no bailouts for credibility. Once people stop trusting your word, everything else becomes more expensive.

The wealthy understand that reputation is not decoration–it is infrastructure. It reduces the need for contracts because your word carries weight. It brings partners to your side when you need them most. It acts as insurance, cushioning you with goodwill during mistakes. In many cases, reputation is worth more than cash, because cash can be raised if reputation is intact. Without reputation, even mountains of cash eventually burn.

Reputation is also an inheritance. The way you conduct yourself today shapes how your children, your partners, or your heirs are received tomorrow. Your name becomes a balance sheet that outlives you. If it carries integrity, it multiplies opportunities across generations. If it carries suspicion, it multiplies obstacles.

Reputation is capital. Treat it with the same seriousness you treat money—because in the end, it buys more than money ever could.

## Rule 26 – Risk is the price of reward

Every reward in finance comes with an invoice. The invoice isn't always obvious, and it rarely arrives at the moment of gain. But it is always there. That invoice is risk.

People often want the upside of investing–growth, returns, compounding–without the downside of volatility, uncertainty, and drawdowns. They ask for the asset that goes up without ever going down, the opportunity that grows without turbulence. Such an asset doesn't exist. The price of reward is enduring periods when the outcome looks uncertain, when you question your own judgment, when headlines scream that this time is different.

The irony is that most people are willing to pay explicit costs–fees, taxes, expenses–because they can see them. But they panic at the implicit cost of risk. A twenty percent market decline feels intolerable, even though it is precisely the price that long-term equity returns demand. The inability to tolerate risk is why many investors buy high and sell low, locking in losses that discipline could have avoided.

Risk is not something to avoid; it is something to respect. Avoid all risk and you avoid all reward. Chase only reward and you invite ruin. The art is in aligning risks with your capacity to endure them. This is why understanding your own psychology matters as much as understanding markets. The right portfolio is not the one with the highest expected return. It is the one whose risks you can actually survive without bailing out at the worst possible moment.

The wealthiest investors don't eliminate risk. They budget for it. They know downturns will come, so they hold cash reserves. They know volatility will strike, so they diversify. They don't treat risk as an accident. They treat it as tuition—the price of admission to the game of reward.

In the end, risk is not a bug of the system. It is the system. If you are not paying it, you are not in line for the reward. The question is not whether you will face risk, but whether you have prepared yourself to pay it without complaint when the bill arrives.

## Rule 27 – Luck is part of every fortune

We love stories of self-made success. They are clean, inspiring, and flattering. But every fortune carries the fingerprints of luck. Right place, right time. The right mentor, the right market cycle, the right regulation, even the right birth. This truth is uncomfortable, because it threatens the narrative of total control. But ignoring luck distorts reality and breeds arrogance.

Luck does not mean effort is irrelevant. Effort matters enormously. Without skill, discipline, and persistence, luck cannot be captured. But to deny luck's role is to misunderstand how unpredictable the world is. A brilliant entrepreneur in a stagnant economy may never be discovered. A mediocre one riding a boom may look like a genius. The line between the two is often thinner than people want to admit.

Acknowledging luck has two benefits. First, it keeps you humble. If success is not solely your doing, arrogance has no foundation. Humility, in turn, protects reputation, relationships, and decision-making. Second, it keeps you empathetic. If your fortune carries strokes of luck, then others' struggles may carry strokes of misfortune. That awareness makes you slower to judge and quicker to understand.

The danger of ignoring luck is overconfidence. When you believe every win is proof of brilliance, you double down recklessly. You take risks your skill cannot cover, assuming the universe owes you more good breaks. Eventually, luck turns–as it always does–and arrogance leaves you exposed.

The wealthiest people rarely deny luck. Many of them admit freely that timing, randomness, and uncontrollable factors played enormous roles in their stories. They still worked hard, but they know others worked just as hard without the same outcomes. This recognition doesn't diminish their effort. It sharpens their perspective.

Luck is part of every fortune. To respect it is not weakness. It is wisdom. It reminds you that wealth is not proof of superiority, and loss is not proof of failure. It keeps you steady when fortune turns against you, and gracious when it turns in your favor.

## Rule 28 – Simplicity beats complexity

Complexity sells. Financial advisors, institutions, and product designers know that if they package something with enough jargon, formulas, and moving parts, people will assume it must be smarter. Complexity flatters the ego—it feels sophisticated to hold what others don't understand. But wealth that endures is rarely complex. It is built on simple principles, repeated consistently.

The paradox is that simplicity is harder than complexity, because it requires clarity. Complexity hides mistakes behind layers of structure; simplicity exposes them. Complexity can be marketed; simplicity must be lived. And simplicity looks boring, which makes it harder to stick with when the world chases excitement.

Think of the most reliable strategies: spend less than you earn, invest regularly, diversify broadly, hold for the long term. These ideas are so simple they can fit on a napkin. Yet they outperform the vast majority of complex systems because they are easier to follow when life gets noisy. The best plan is not the one that looks brilliant in theory. It is the one you can keep doing in practice, through booms and busts.

Complexity has another hidden cost: it erodes understanding. When you don't fully understand what you own, you can't tell whether it's working or broken. You end up outsourcing conviction to others, which makes you fragile in a crisis. Simplicity keeps conviction in your own hands. If you know what you own and why you own it, you can hold through volatility while others panic.

This is not to say complexity never works. Some investors thrive on sophisticated strategies. But for most people, complexity is camouflage for confusion. The lesson is clear: wealth doesn't reward how clever you look. It rewards how consistent you are. And consistency comes easier when the plan is simple enough to survive your own doubts.

Simplicity beats complexity because it aligns with human nature. It doesn't require perfect discipline, just repeatable habits. It doesn't crumble under stress, because it doesn't depend on fragile assumptions. The future is uncertain, but simplicity is robust across many scenarios. Complexity is fragile to one wrong detail.

In the end, the wealthiest are not those with the most complicated spreadsheets. They are those with a system so simple it works when everything else is chaos.

## Rule 29 – Control is more valuable than income

Income impresses. Control liberates. Most people spend their lives chasing bigger paychecks, believing that more income is the ultimate sign of wealth. But income without control is a golden cage. You may earn a fortune, but if you cannot decide how to spend your time, where to live, or which people to avoid, you are not free.

Control is subtle. It doesn't show up in a salary figure or a net worth statement. It shows up in the ability to say no. To turn down a client who doesn't respect you. To walk away from a job that drains you. To take a day off without fear of collapse. That is why control is more valuable than income: it defines the quality of your daily life, not just the size of your bank account.

Many high earners quietly admit they feel trapped. They cannot downshift because their lifestyle has scaled with their paycheck. They cannot leave because they are bound by contracts, obligations, or debt. Their income looks powerful but it owns them. Contrast that with someone who earns less but structures life around autonomy. The latter might not impress at a dinner party, but they live more truly wealthy.

The psychology here is critical. Chasing income often feels endless, because there is always someone earning more. Chasing control feels finite, because it is defined by personal thresholds. You may not be able to catch every millionaire above you, but you can design a life where no one else dictates your mornings. That is a race you can win.

Control also compounds. Each decision that increases autonomy creates room for better decisions tomorrow. Control over your calendar lets you rest, which improves your judgment. Control over your environment shields you from toxic pressures, which extends your career. Control over spending prevents debt, which preserves freedom. These effects multiply quietly until you realize you have built a fortress more valuable than the highest paycheck you ever dreamed of.

In the end, income measures how much others value your time. Control measures how much you value your own. When the two conflict, control is the wealth that lasts.

## Rule 30 – Inflation is the silent thief

Inflation rarely makes headlines in the same way stock crashes or housing bubbles do. It doesn't announce itself with panic–it creeps in quietly, eroding wealth one small slice at a time. That is why it is so dangerous. A crisis you can see makes you react. Inflation steals in slow motion, and by the time you notice, the damage is already done.

At its core, inflation is simple: the same money buys less over time. But psychologically, it is profound. You work, save, and invest with the assumption that your future dollars will hold their power. When inflation rises, that assumption breaks. Your savings account that once felt like security now feels like a melting ice cube. A bond that seemed safe turns into a guaranteed loss. The real return–the only return that matters–is exposed.

The silent nature of inflation makes people underestimate it. A three percent inflation rate sounds harmless. But over twenty years, it halves the purchasing power of your money. It doesn't just affect luxuries–it affects rent, food, education, healthcare. It doesn't just punish the careless–it punishes anyone who forgets that cash is not neutral.

The lesson is not to fear inflation, but to respect it. Protect yourself by owning assets that grow faster than prices: equities, real estate, productive businesses. Keep cash for liquidity, but recognize that cash is a short-term tool, not a long-term store of value. Understand that stability on paper is not always stability in reality.

Inflation is also a reminder that standing still is moving backward. Doing nothing with your money is not safety–it is surrender.

The silent thief collects from everyone, but the bill is highest for those who believed they were safe by avoiding all risk.

# Rule 31 – Expenses define you more than income

Most people measure financial success by income. They ask, "How much do you make?" as if the answer reveals the whole story. But income is only half the equation. Expenses decide the rest. Two people can earn the same salary—one feels secure, the other feels suffocated. The difference is not what comes in. It's what goes out.

Expenses define you because they shape your margin of freedom. A high income paired with higher expenses leaves nothing. A modest income paired with disciplined expenses creates surplus. Surplus is the engine of wealth. Without it, you can work your whole life and end with little more than exhaustion. With it, you can build assets, endure shocks, and eventually buy back your time.

The danger of expenses is that they rise invisibly with lifestyle. A raise feels like freedom, but it tempts you into upgrades—bigger houses, nicer cars, better vacations—that quickly become fixed costs. What felt optional becomes baseline. And once baseline shifts, stepping back feels like loss, even if the new baseline is unsustainable. That is how golden handcuffs are forged: income may rise, but expenses tighten the chains.

Psychologically, managing expenses is harder than earning more. Society celebrates income. It rewards the visible success of titles, salaries, and bonuses. It does not reward the quiet restraint of living below your means. That makes it easy to justify indulgence and hard to celebrate discipline. Yet discipline is what creates resilience. Expenses are not just numbers on a budget—they are commitments that shape your future.

Wealth is not defined by the size of your paycheck. It is defined by the spread between what you earn and what you spend. That spread, protected and repeated, is the true measure of financial strength. Expenses, not income, are what reveal whether you are free or merely busy.

# Rule 32 – Wealth without purpose is emptiness

Money can solve problems. It can buy comfort, security, and time. But once those needs are met, wealth without a deeper purpose begins to feel hollow. History is filled with examples of people who achieved enormous financial success only to find themselves restless, anxious, or even depressed. They discovered too late that numbers alone cannot carry meaning.

Purpose is what transforms wealth from accumulation into fulfillment. Without purpose, money becomes a scoreboard that never stops running. Every milestone leads only to the question: what's next? That endless chase creates anxiety instead of freedom. But with purpose–supporting family, building a legacy, creating opportunities, advancing causes that matter–wealth takes on a direction. It becomes a tool for building, not just a shield for hoarding.

The danger of ignoring purpose is that wealth then serves only ego. You buy things not because they matter, but because they signal status. You pursue growth not because you need it, but because you fear looking small next to someone else. Eventually, the performance becomes exhausting. True satisfaction never arrives because you were measuring the wrong thing.

Purpose is deeply personal. For some, it is raising children with opportunities they never had. For others, it is supporting their community, creating art, or funding research. It does not have to be noble in anyone else's eyes–it only has to be meaningful in yours. The critical point is that wealth without this anchor drifts into emptiness.

Wealth is not the destination. It is the amplifier. If you have purpose, wealth magnifies it. If you don't, wealth magnifies the void.

## Rule 33 – Paper beats memory

Human memory is fragile. We forget details, misremember timelines, and edit stories to suit emotions. Money, contracts, and obligations don't tolerate that fragility. That is why paper—records, agreements, written plans—beats memory every time.

A handshake feels noble, but disputes rarely respect handshakes. An agreement committed to writing provides clarity when recollection blurs. A budget tracked on paper exposes spending habits that memory downplays. An investment plan written in advance keeps you steady when fear or greed tries to rewrite your rules. Paper is not just documentation. It is discipline externalized.

The danger of relying on memory is that memory bends to emotion. In bull markets, you "always believed" prices would rise. In bear markets, you "knew all along" disaster was coming. In arguments, you remember the facts that suit your story and forget the rest. Paper anchors you to reality. It keeps a record that does not change when your emotions do.

The wealthy understand this. They document wills, trusts, contracts, and policies not because they distrust people, but because they distrust memory. They keep records of decisions to avoid costly reinventions. They treat paper as insurance against forgetfulness and as protection against dispute.

There is also a psychological benefit. When your plans are written, they feel real. A vague intention to save is just a thought. A written plan to save a fixed amount each month, signed and tracked, becomes a contract with yourself. And people tend to keep contracts more reliably than they keep promises whispered in their own head.

Paper beats memory because money demands clarity. If you rely on recollection, you will bend the story until it fits your mood. If you rely on paper, you face the truth—even when it is uncomfortable. And facing the truth is the first step to building wealth that lasts.

## Rule 34 – Systems survive mood swings

Wealth is not built in moments of perfect clarity. It is built in the messy middle–when fear is loud, when greed is tempting, when fatigue whispers to quit. In those moments, moods are unreliable. If your financial life depends on how you feel in a given week, it will not last. Systems are the antidote.

A system is a plan that does not care how you feel. Automatic savings, standing investment orders, written spending rules, pre-set asset allocations–these are structures that keep moving even when your motivation stalls. The brilliance of a system is that it replaces decision with design. Instead of asking every month, "Do I feel like saving?" the system saves for you. Instead of wondering, "Should I invest today?" the system does it on schedule.

Most people underestimate how powerful moods are. When markets rise, greed makes us abandon caution. When they fall, fear convinces us to sell at the worst possible moment. Moods swing faster than logic. But systems don't swing. They are boring, repetitive, and predictable–and precisely because of that, they are stronger than our emotions.

Consider the investor who relies on mood. When markets are calm, he saves and invests. When markets panic, he hesitates or sells. Over decades, his returns lag because he bought and sold at the worst times. Contrast this with the investor who set up automatic contributions and refused to interfere. She may not have the sharpest instincts, but she didn't need them. Her system protected her from her moods, and compounding rewarded her patience.

Systems look rigid, but in reality they are liberating. They free you from the exhausting burden of constant decision-making. They let you live your life without financial anxiety dominating every thought. And most importantly, they keep you in the game long enough for wealth to emerge.

In finance, moods are weather. Systems are climate. Weather changes daily. Climate endures.

## Rule 35 – Foundations outlive strategies

Every generation believes it has discovered the perfect strategy–new formulas, new structures, new hacks to outsmart risk. Some of these strategies work for a while. Many collapse. What survives are not the tactics of the moment, but the foundations underneath them.

The foundations are simple truths: spend less than you earn, save before you spend, protect before you grow, respect risk, value reputation, and define enough. These principles have worked across centuries, currencies, and regimes. Strategies–specific funds, industries, or schemes–rise and fall. Foundations endure.

The danger is mistaking fashion for foundation. People chase the latest investment vehicle or tax loophole, convinced they've found the secret. But fashions expire. The core truths of wealth do not. Protect your downside, and you will outlast downturns. Live below your means, and you will accumulate. Focus on freedom, and you will stay motivated. These are not strategies. They are laws.

Foundations also act as anchors. They keep you steady when strategies fail, because strategies always fail sometimes. The investor who built on foundations may lose in one cycle, but survives to win in the next. The one who built only on strategies often doesn't survive at all.

In the end, the wealthiest are not those with the cleverest playbook. They are those who respected the unchanging foundations and allowed strategies to orbit around them. Foundations outlive strategies. That is why they deserve your focus.

## Rule 36 – Fear sells faster than hope

Fear has always traveled faster than hope. It is hardwired into us. Our ancestors survived not by being optimistic, but by overreacting to danger. If you ran every time you heard a rustle in the bushes, you might look foolish nine times out of ten. But the tenth time–the one where the rustle was a predator–your fear saved you. That instinct is still in us. Which is why financial fear, even when exaggerated, spreads like wildfire.

Turn on the news. Headlines about crashes, recessions, and bubbles dominate. Warnings of collapse attract more clicks than stories of steady growth. People will always stop to look at the burning building, not the one that stands quietly intact. Fear is dramatic. Hope is quiet. And drama sells.

The result is that investors often drown in noise that exaggerates risk. Every downturn is "the big one." Every correction is "the end." Yet history shows that markets have endured wars, depressions, pandemics, and political crises–again and again–while continuing their long upward climb. The fearful stories spread faster, but the hopeful trajectory lasted longer.

The danger is not just external. Fear changes behavior. It makes you sell low, hoard cash, and abandon plans. It convinces you that safety today is more important than growth tomorrow. Fear whispers that your situation is different, that the rules no longer apply, that this time really is the end. And because fear spreads so quickly, it can become self-fulfilling. Panics cause the very collapses they predicted.

The antidote is perspective. Acknowledge fear—because it will always come—but frame it against history. Ask: is this fear revealing a real structural collapse, or is it another headline exploiting instinct? Hope takes longer to prove itself, but over decades it has always been the better bet.

Fear will always sell faster than hope. But you don't have to buy it.

## Rule 37 – Greed never sleeps

Fear comes in spikes, but greed hums constantly in the background. Unlike fear, which paralyzes, greed propels. It whispers that you could have more, that you deserve more, that you will be left behind if you don't chase more. And because it never rests, it can wear down even the most disciplined investor.

Greed doesn't always look like greed. Sometimes it looks like ambition, optimism, or simple excitement. You tell yourself you're just being proactive, that you're maximizing opportunity. But underneath, the impulse is the same: the belief that what you have is never enough, that more is always just around the corner.

The market exploits this perfectly. Every bull run is fueled by greed disguised as confidence. People stop asking whether valuations make sense and start asking why they don't own more of the thing that's going up. Friends become millionaires overnight, neighbors boast of quick profits, and greed whispers that sitting still is failure. Unlike fear, which can be contained by withdrawing, greed spreads precisely because it feels good.

The danger of greed is not just financial loss. It is distortion of judgment. Greed convinces you to ignore risks, to stretch leverage, to trust people you shouldn't, to abandon strategies that worked because they now feel "too slow." It convinces you that your recent gains prove permanent skill, when in reality they may be temporary luck. And when greed runs unchecked, it usually ends in the same place: collapse.

Yet greed is also a paradox. Without it, progress slows. The desire for more drives innovation, risk-taking, and expansion. Greed, in its tempered form, is ambition. But ambition without brakes becomes greed in its pure form—relentless, restless, destructive.

The lesson is not to kill greed. It cannot be killed. The lesson is to recognize its voice, to know that it never sleeps, and to decide in advance how far you will let it take you. Because unchecked, it will take everything.

## Rule 38 – Envy destroys silently

Envy doesn't announce itself the way fear or greed do. It creeps in quietly, almost invisibly, until it shapes your behavior without you realizing it. You see a colleague with a better car, a neighbor with a bigger house, a peer who "made it" faster, and suddenly your own progress feels small. Nothing in your life changed–except the comparison. And that comparison has the power to poison everything.

The danger of envy is that it makes success feel inadequate. A raise that thrilled you last year now feels like an insult because someone else got more. A portfolio you were proud of suddenly looks pitiful because a friend's speculative gamble doubled overnight. Envy erodes joy not by taking away what you have, but by making you blind to it.

Unlike greed, envy doesn't drive you forward–it corrodes from within. It pushes you to chase things you don't even want, just to prove you can. It tempts you into risks you don't understand, debts you can't afford, and sacrifices that leave you emptier than before. And because envy is quiet, you rarely admit it's there. You rationalize your choices as ambition or competitiveness, when in truth you are simply measuring yourself against someone else's ruler.

The tragedy is that envy never ends. There is always someone with more–more money, more recognition, more freedom. If your satisfaction depends on winning every comparison, you will never win at all. The antidote is to redefine the game. Instead of asking, "Do I have more than them?" ask, "Do I have enough for me?" The first question leads to exhaustion. The second leads to peace.

Wealth without freedom from envy is a prison disguised as success. The richest people in the world can still feel poor if they let others set the standard. Envy destroys silently because it convinces you to abandon your own definition of wealth. And once you do that, no amount will ever be enough.

## Rule 39 – Loss feels twice as heavy as gain

Human beings are not wired to weigh wins and losses equally. Psychologists call it *loss aversion*: the pain of losing is about twice as powerful as the joy of gaining. This imbalance is not a quirk–it's survival instinct. Our ancestors could celebrate a good hunt, but one mistake could mean starvation. Evolution taught us to fear losses more than we value gains. That wiring still governs how we handle money.

In investing, this shows up everywhere. A $10,000 gain feels good, but a $10,000 loss feels unbearable. Investors who see red numbers on a screen often panic, even if the long-term plan is intact. That panic leads to selling at lows, abandoning strategies, and locking in losses that patience would have reversed. The market rewards those who can endure pain, but pain is precisely what most people are least equipped to endure.

Loss aversion also explains why insurance sells, why people hoard cash, why they resist risks even when odds are in their favor. The prospect of losing dominates rational calculations. We don't ask, "What is the most likely outcome?" We ask, "What is the worst possible outcome?" and then avoid it at all costs.

The irony is that the same instinct that once kept us alive now limits our potential. Avoiding all losses means avoiding the risks that create wealth. The market is a machine that transfers money from the impatient to the patient, from those who can't endure temporary losses to those who can.

But the lesson isn't to ignore pain–it's to expect it. If you understand that losses will always feel heavier, you can design systems to protect yourself from overreacting. Automate contributions. Diversify. Write down your plan in advance. The goal is not to stop feeling losses—they will always hurt. The goal is to keep that hurt from making the decision for you.

Loss feels twice as heavy as gain, but the ability to live with that imbalance is what separates those who build wealth from those who abandon it at the worst moment.

## Rule 40 – The crowd is usually wrong

There is comfort in numbers. If everyone is buying, it feels safe to buy. If everyone is selling, it feels smart to sell. Following the crowd lowers the anxiety of being wrong alone. But history is brutal on crowds: they are usually wrong at the moments that matter most.

Every bubble is a story of crowds. Tulip mania, dot-com stocks, housing in 2008—the pattern repeats. Prices rise, more people join, and the rising price becomes its own justification. Nobody wants to be left out, so more money floods in. At the peak, when the crowd feels most confident, risk is highest. And when the collapse comes, the same crowd stampedes in the other direction, selling at the worst possible time.

The irony is that the crowd is not irrational in the moment. Each individual thinks they are safe because everyone else is doing the same thing. Safety in numbers works in nature—herds protect against predators. But in markets, the herd is the predator. By the time the crowd arrives, the opportunity is usually gone, and what remains is fragility disguised as safety.

This doesn't mean the crowd is always wrong about direction—sometimes they are right. It means they are usually wrong about timing. The crowd buys after most of the upside has already happened, and sells after most of the downside is already over. The lesson is not to assume you are smarter than everyone else. The lesson is to recognize that comfort in numbers is often a trap.

Wealth is rarely built by joining the crowd at its loudest moments. It is built by standing apart long enough to survive the noise.

The crowd is usually wrong not because people are stupid, but because people are human—and humans crave belonging more than they crave accuracy.

## Rule 41 – Timing is luck, not genius

Everyone wants to believe they can time the market. Buy low, sell high—it sounds so simple, so logical, so rewarding. And every once in a while, someone gets it right. They buy at the bottom, sell at the top, and tell the story for years. It looks like genius. But in truth, it was luck.

Markets are complex systems shaped by billions of decisions, geopolitical shocks, technological shifts, and human psychology. Predicting exact tops and bottoms is like predicting the precise second a volcano will erupt. You might guess right once, but repeatability is near impossible. And repeatability is what separates skill from luck.

The danger is that people mistake luck for genius. They get one call right and assume they've cracked the code. Then they start betting bigger, convinced of their own insight. Inevitably, they are wrong the next time, and the losses erase the earlier gains. The history of investing is filled with people who were "right once" and built careers—or destroyed fortunes—on that illusion.

The irony is that you don't need perfect timing to build wealth. Time in the market matters far more than timing the market. A steady, disciplined investor who buys consistently and holds through cycles will usually outperform the market timer who guesses right once and wrong often. The math of compounding rewards patience, not precision.

The wealthy understand this. They don't waste energy trying to call exact tops or bottoms. They focus on owning durable assets, managing risk, and surviving downturns. They let time do the work. Genius is overrated; endurance is undefeated.

Timing feels like genius when it works. But over the long run, it's luck. And building wealth on luck is not a strategy. It's a gamble.

## Rule 42 – Patience is the hardest investment

Markets reward patience, but patience is the rarest commodity. Everyone knows that compounding works best over decades, that businesses need years to mature, that wealth is a long game. Yet knowing is not the same as doing. The hardest part of investing is not understanding the math. It's sitting still long enough for the math to work.

Patience is hard because the world is noisy. Headlines scream about crises and opportunities. Friends boast of quick wins. Social media turns investing into a contest of instant gratification. Against that backdrop, holding steady looks naïve. You feel like you're falling behind if you're not constantly making moves. The irony is that constant motion is usually what destroys returns.

Think of a tree. You don't dig it up every week to check if it's growing. You plant it, water it, and wait. Yet in finance, people do the opposite. They uproot their investments at the first sign of doubt, killing the compounding before it has time to show. Patience means resisting the urge to interfere. It means accepting boredom as a feature, not a flaw.

The wealthiest investors are not those with the best stock picks. They are those who could sit through decades of uncertainty without abandoning their plan. They understand that the short term is noise, the long term is signal. Patience is less about IQ than about temperament. It is emotional stamina disguised as financial wisdom.

In a world obsessed with speed, patience feels radical. But wealth is not a sprint. It is a marathon you win simply by refusing to stop running.

# Rule 43 – Confidence without discipline is ruin

Confidence is seductive. It makes you bold, decisive, willing to take risks others avoid. In moderation, confidence is necessary—without it, you never invest, never build, never take the leap. But confidence without discipline is gasoline without brakes. It burns hot, fast, and often ends in destruction.

Many fortunes have been lost by people who were brilliant and confident, but lacked discipline. They believed so strongly in their own ideas that they ignored warning signs, dismissed critics, and doubled down on mistakes. Confidence told them they couldn't fail. Reality reminded them otherwise.

Discipline is what keeps confidence in check. It is the system of limits you set in advance: diversification, risk management, position sizing, stop-losses, or simply the humility to say, "I might be wrong." Discipline forces you to operate within boundaries, even when your confidence tempts you to go further. Without discipline, confidence becomes arrogance. And arrogance in finance is eventually punished.

The paradox is that confidence and discipline must coexist. Too little confidence, and you never act. Too little discipline, and your actions destroy you. The balance is rare but essential. The most successful investors don't silence their confidence—they pair it with systems that protect them from themselves.

Confidence builds fortunes. Discipline preserves them. Lose the second, and the first becomes a ticking clock.

## Rule 44 – Certainty is an illusion

Humans crave certainty. We want to believe that experts can predict markets, that models can forecast economies, that trends can be mapped with precision. Certainty feels safe. It gives us the illusion of control in a world full of randomness. But the truth is uncomfortable: certainty in finance is an illusion.

Markets are not equations; they are ecosystems of billions of people making decisions under uncertainty. A single event–a war, a new technology, a pandemic–can render the most elegant forecast worthless. Yet people keep paying for predictions, because uncertainty is unbearable. We would rather have a wrong answer than no answer at all.

The danger of chasing certainty is that it leads to overconfidence. You anchor on forecasts and ignore evidence to the contrary. You build fragile strategies that assume the future will look exactly like your models. When reality diverges–as it always does–the collapse feels shocking, even though uncertainty was the rule all along.

The wise don't seek certainty. They seek resilience. They design systems that survive a range of outcomes, not just the one they hope for. They diversify, keep liquidity, and avoid leverage that depends on perfect conditions. They accept that forecasts are entertainment, not guarantees.

The irony is that accepting uncertainty makes you more certain of survival. Once you stop pretending you can predict, you start preparing for what you cannot predict. And that preparation is what actually builds lasting wealth. Certainty is an illusion. Survival is reality.

## Rule 45 – FOMO is the modern tax

Every generation invents a new way to charge people for impatience. Today it's called FOMO—the fear of missing out. It is the tax you pay when you chase what everyone else is chasing, not because you understand it, but because you're terrified of being left behind.

FOMO whispers that your steady plan is too slow, that your modest gains are pathetic, that your discipline is costing you fortune. It points to your neighbor who "made a killing" in crypto, your colleague who flipped houses, the influencer who retired at thirty. It convinces you that if you don't jump in now, you'll miss the train forever.

The result is predictable. You buy at the top, because that's when the noise is loudest. You sell at the bottom, because that's when fear takes over. Each round-trip becomes a transfer of wealth from the impatient to the patient. That transfer is the FOMO tax, and it is one of the most expensive in finance.

The tragedy is that FOMO never ends. Even if you catch one wave, another will appear, and you'll feel poor again by comparison. Chasing trends becomes an endless loop of excitement and regret. The more you pay the FOMO tax, the less capital you have to invest in strategies that actually work.

The antidote is perspective. Remember that wealth is not a race. Missing one opportunity does not matter if you are positioned to capture the next ten. History rewards those who avoided collapse, not those who caught every boom. The market is a marathon, not a sprint, and FOMO is the tax collected from those who can't stop sprinting.

The wealthy don't avoid FOMO by being immune to envy. They avoid it by remembering the cost. Every time they feel the urge to chase, they ask: am I about to pay another invisible tax? Most people never stop to ask. And that silence is how fortunes slip away.

# Rule 46 – People remember stories, not numbers

Numbers are precise. They are charts, ratios, percentages, probabilities. They belong to spreadsheets and reports. But when it comes to human behavior, numbers rarely move people. Stories do.

This is why markets are driven as much by narratives as by data. Investors don't just buy earnings–they buy the story of a company transforming the world. Nations don't just respond to statistics–they respond to the story those numbers suggest about prosperity or decline. Even personal finance is less about math than about meaning: you save not because of a percentage on a page, but because of the story you tell yourself about freedom, family, or the future.

The irony is that stories can both illuminate and deceive. They can simplify complex truths into something memorable, which helps us act. But they can also seduce us into ignoring data entirely. The tech boom of the 1990s was powered by a story: the internet will change everything. That story was true, but the valuations it justified were absurd. Investors who bought the story without discipline paid dearly.

This is not an argument against stories. It is a reminder that stories are the language of memory. Numbers fade. People forget the exact figures of inflation in the 1970s, but they remember the story of long gas lines and economic malaise. Investors forget precise quarterly earnings, but remember the story of Apple rising from near bankruptcy to the world's most valuable company.

If you want to persuade, teach, or lead, you need stories. And if you want to protect yourself, you must learn to separate the power of a story from the truth of the numbers behind it. Because in the end, your brain will cling to the story, not the spreadsheet.

## Rule 47 – The bigger the ego, the weaker the fortress

Wealth and ego have an uneasy relationship. Success inflates confidence, and confidence, left unchecked, inflates ego. The problem is that ego craves recognition more than resilience. It pushes people to take risks, not for the sake of returns, but for the sake of appearing brilliant. And that is how fortresses crumble.

The bigger the ego, the harder it is to accept limits. Ego says, "I can't be wrong." Ego says, "The rules don't apply to me." Ego says, "If I stop now, people will think I failed." These voices drive people to double down on bad bets, to over-leverage, to refuse diversification, to chase status symbols. Ego doesn't just weaken defenses–it actively dismantles them.

The strongest fortresses are built on humility. They are filled with redundancies, margins of safety, and acceptance of uncertainty. They don't need to prove anything to outsiders, so they don't take unnecessary risks to impress. They value survival over spectacle. Ego hates this, because humility looks small in the short run. But in the long run, humility keeps the fortress standing while ego-rich empires fall.

History is littered with examples. Titans of industry who believed themselves untouchable, only to be undone by hubris. Investors who ignored warning signs because acknowledging them would bruise their pride. Families who lived beyond their means to display success, only to collapse under the weight of debt. In every case, the ego was bigger than the foundation.

Wealth without ego is quiet, boring, invisible. It prioritizes endurance over applause. Wealth with ego is noisy, fragile, and temporary. The lesson is simple: the bigger the ego, the weaker the fortress. If you want your wealth to last, build it on humility—not on the need to be admired.

## Rule 48 – Security feels boring until you lose it

Security rarely excites anyone. It doesn't give you a rush, it doesn't trend on social media, and it doesn't make for good conversation at dinner parties. A fully funded emergency account, a conservative portfolio allocation, or insurance coverage sound dull compared to stories of ten-baggers or moonshot startups. Security feels boring–until the moment it's gone.

When things are calm, security looks like wasted opportunity. Why hold cash that earns little when markets are booming? Why pay insurance premiums if you've never filed a claim? Why settle for steady but modest growth when others seem to be doubling their money? The temptation to abandon security in pursuit of excitement is constant. And for a while, it even looks smart–right up until reality reminds you why security mattered.

The moment you lose security, boredom transforms into desperation. A layoff without savings. A medical bill without insurance. A margin call that forces you to sell assets you love at fire-sale prices. Suddenly, the quiet safety net you dismissed as boring reveals itself as priceless. Security is invisible until it disappears.

The paradox is that security compounds invisibly, too. Every crisis you avoid because you had reserves is a silent victory. Every mistake you survive because you had margin is a compounding event–your wealth keeps growing because it wasn't wiped out. The most successful investors and families aren't necessarily the boldest. They are the ones who treated security as non-negotiable, even when it felt dull.

Security may never feel exciting. But it is the stage on which all excitement plays out. Without it, every risk becomes existential. With it, risks become manageable, recoverable, survivable. Security is not boring. It is the quiet foundation of freedom.

## Rule 49 – Shortcuts cost more in the end

The promise of a shortcut is irresistible: faster results, easier gains, a way around the hard work. In wealth, shortcuts often appear as get-rich-quick schemes, insider tips, or overly complex financial products that promise high returns with low risk. They all share one thing in common: they sound too good to be true because they are.

Shortcuts cost more in the end because they trade discipline for illusion. They lure you with stories of others who "made it big overnight," convincing you that you, too, can skip the boring grind of saving, investing, and compounding. But compounding has no shortcut. It requires time, patience, and repetition. Every attempt to bypass that reality ends up costing more–through losses, fees, or missed opportunities.

The psychology of shortcuts is rooted in impatience. People hate the idea of waiting decades for compounding to work. They crave immediacy, even if it means higher risk. But impatience is expensive. It pushes you into investments you don't understand, leverage you can't manage, and schemes that collapse at the first sign of stress. By the time you learn the lesson, the shortcut has turned into the longest, most painful path of all.

History is full of examples. From speculative bubbles to Ponzi schemes, the victims were not unintelligent–they were impatient. They wanted to skip the slow part of wealth-building, forgetting that the slow part is the point. The irony is that true wealth is built on the very habits shortcuts try to avoid: saving consistently, investing wisely, waiting patiently.

Shortcuts cost more because they destroy the two things wealth depends on: capital and trust. Lose money, and you can rebuild. Lose trust—in yourself, in your judgment, in your discipline—and rebuilding becomes even harder.

The lesson is simple: there are no shortcuts. The long road is the only road. And once you accept that, the temptation to take detours fades. The cost of shortcuts is too high, because they charge the one thing you can't replace: time.

## Rule 50 – Stress compounds faster than money

Everyone knows that money compounds. Fewer people realize that stress does too. And while financial compounding builds freedom, stress compounding erodes it. Each financial decision you make either adds resilience to your life or adds pressure. Over time, the pressure multiplies in ways as destructive as high-interest debt.

Stress compounds because it never arrives alone. A risky investment that goes wrong doesn't just cost money–it costs sleep. A lifestyle inflated by debt doesn't just demand higher payments–it demands constant worry about keeping up. A fragile job, a toxic partnership, a dependence on luck–each adds a layer of strain. And like interest on interest, those layers interact, magnifying the weight until it becomes unbearable.

The cruelest part is that stress compounds invisibly. You think you're just making one compromise–taking on a little more debt, ignoring a warning sign, overextending slightly. At first, nothing breaks. But the strain builds silently, eroding health, relationships, and judgment. By the time you notice, the compounding has already taken hold.

Money can be rebuilt. Stress, once compounded, leaves scars. Chronic anxiety shortens horizons. Exhaustion leads to bad decisions, which create more stress, which lead to worse decisions. It is a feedback loop that accelerates downward, often faster than wealth can grow upward.

The antidote is margin. Build buffers not just in your finances, but in your life. Cash reserves reduce financial stress. Healthy boundaries reduce relational stress. Diversification reduces career stress. Simplicity reduces cognitive stress. Each margin may look like inefficiency in the short term, but in the long term, it stops the compounding of pressure before it crushes you.

Money compounds. But so does stress. And unless you guard against it, the second can cancel out the benefits of the first.

## Rule 51 – Happiness has no market price

Markets can put a price on almost anything–stocks, bonds, commodities, real estate. They can measure returns, cash flows, and yields with precision. But there is no ticker symbol for happiness. No exchange lists contentment. And yet, happiness is the real endgame of wealth. Everything else is a means to that end.

The mistake people make is assuming happiness scales automatically with money. They think another raise, another house, another zero in the account will finally unlock it. For a while, it works–upgrades feel good. But soon, the feeling fades, and the bar moves higher. The cycle repeats until wealth becomes a treadmill of dissatisfaction.

Happiness resists market logic because it is rooted in meaning, not numbers. Time with loved ones. Work that aligns with values. Freedom to choose your days. Health that allows you to enjoy what you've built. These don't have market prices, yet they determine whether wealth feels abundant or empty.

The irony is that the market will try to sell you substitutes–luxury goods, status symbols, fleeting experiences. These can be bought, but they often deliver less happiness than promised. True happiness is quieter. It looks like security, relationships, purpose, and peace of mind. None of these can be purchased directly, though money can create the conditions for them.

The wealthiest people are not those with the most toys. They are those who figured out how to translate money into happiness–and stopped when the translation no longer worked. They know that happiness has no market price because it cannot be traded, borrowed, or speculated on. It must be cultivated.

Money can buy many things, but it cannot buy the feeling that enough is enough. Happiness begins where the market ends.

## Rule 52 – Scarcity creates value

Abundance is deceptive. When something is everywhere, we stop noticing it. When it disappears, we realize how much it mattered. This is as true with money as it is with time, health, and opportunity. Scarcity is what forces us to value, prioritize, and protect. Without it, we drift. With it, we focus.

The psychology of scarcity explains why people save water in a drought but waste it when reservoirs are full. It explains why limited-time offers drive sales, why rare art commands prices far above its intrinsic cost, and why people guard their last dollar more fiercely than their first thousand. Scarcity sharpens attention in ways abundance never can.

Wealth complicates this dynamic. The more money you have, the less scarce it feels. That abundance can dull discipline. You stop noticing expenses, stop questioning investments, stop valuing the margin that got you here. Slowly, abundance erodes resilience. The irony is that the wealthier you become, the more deliberate you must be in creating artificial scarcity–budgets, boundaries, rules–so that you don't destroy what abundance built.

Scarcity also reveals what really matters. When time feels endless, you waste it. When you realize it is finite, you cherish it. Money works the same way. If you had infinite capital, you'd lose track of meaning. But with limits, you must choose. Those choices–how you allocate scarce resources–are what define your life more than the size of your account ever will.

Scarcity creates value because it forces perspective. It reminds us that nothing–money, health, time, trust–is truly limitless. Treating resources as scarce, even when they are abundant, is how wealth survives the very abundance that threatens it.

## Rule 53 – Trust is a currency

Every transaction involves more than money. It involves trust. A client hires you not just for your service, but because they trust you'll deliver. An investor backs a company not just for its product, but because they trust the team. Banks, partnerships, even families–none of them function without trust. It is the invisible currency that underpins all visible currencies.

Trust is valuable because it lowers friction. Without it, every deal requires thick contracts, constant oversight, and costly enforcement. With it, agreements move faster, cheaper, and smoother. Trust compounds like capital: the more you earn, the easier it is to earn more. Break it, and you start from zero–or worse, from negative.

The paradox of trust is that it takes years to build and moments to destroy. A single breach–a missed payment, a broken promise, a careless lie–can erase decades of goodwill. And unlike money, trust has no central bank. Once it's gone, you can't print more. You must rebuild slowly, transaction by transaction, promise by promise.

The wealthiest understand that trust is not decoration–it's infrastructure. Reputation, reliability, discretion: these are assets as valuable as stocks or property. In many cases, they're worth more. Cash can be raised if trust is intact. But with no trust, even mountains of cash lose their power, because nobody will transact with you.

Trust is also intergenerational. A family name built on integrity becomes a passport that opens doors for children and grandchildren. A name built on dishonesty becomes a burden they must carry. Money may not last generations. Trust, if preserved, often does.

Trust is a currency. Earn it carefully, spend it wisely, and protect it fiercely. Because unlike money, once lost, it may never return.

## Rule 54 – Laws change, principles endure

It's easy to mistake the legal code for the foundation of wealth. People build fortunes around tax loopholes, subsidies, favorable regulations, and political winds. And sometimes those strategies work–until they don't. Because laws change. Politicians rewrite rules. Courts reinterpret them. A strategy that feels permanent today may be illegal tomorrow.

History is full of examples. Tax shelters that once attracted billions were dismantled overnight. Entire industries–from alcohol to cannabis, from crypto to banking–have flipped from forbidden to mainstream or back again, depending on the pen of a legislator. If your wealth depends solely on laws staying the same, you are betting against history. Laws are temporary scaffolding.

Principles, however, endure. Spend less than you earn. Protect before you grow. Diversify across risks you don't control. Own assets that produce real value. These are not dependent on the whims of policy. They worked a century ago, they work now, and they will work a century from now.

The wealthy who last don't ignore laws–they adapt to them. They use the rules of the day, but they never confuse them with permanence. Their true foundation rests on principles that survive political shifts. They know the difference between a tactic and a truth.

Chasing laws is a game of speed. Living by principles is a game of endurance. When the rules change, those who relied only on tactics scramble. Those who built on principles remain standing.

## Rule 55 – Borders define opportunity

Wealth is not evenly distributed, because opportunity is not evenly distributed. Borders–geographic, political, cultural–shape where and how money can be made. The same skill or business that thrives in one country may struggle in another, not because the idea is bad, but because the border changes the rules of the game.

Borders define tax regimes, labor markets, currencies, and legal protections. They decide whether capital flows freely or is trapped, whether innovation is rewarded or punished, whether contracts are enforced or ignored. To ignore borders is to assume the world is flat. It isn't.

But borders are more than lines on maps. They are also psychological. The borders of your network, your language, your comfort zone–they define what you perceive as possible. Someone who never crosses them will assume opportunity is scarce. Someone who does learns that wealth is often a matter of jurisdiction, not genius.

The wealthy pay attention to borders because they know they create asymmetry. A company incorporated in one place but operating in another can legally reduce taxes. An individual who understands visa and residency systems can unlock access to markets closed to others. A family that diversifies across borders protects itself from political instability at home.

The paradox of borders is that they both limit and liberate. They restrict you if you stay inside them blindly. They expand you if you learn how to navigate across them. Wealth multiplies not just by what you know, but by where you are allowed to apply it.

Borders define opportunity because they shape the playing field. Those who see them as walls stay confined. Those who see them as doors step into rooms others don't even know exist.

## Rule 56 – Paperwork is power

Most people see paperwork as bureaucracy–tedious forms, signatures, and stamps that slow things down. But in wealth, paperwork is power. It turns intentions into enforceable rights, conversations into contracts, and assets into legally recognized property. Without paperwork, ownership is fragile. With it, ownership becomes protected by the weight of an entire system.

Think of land. For centuries, people worked fields they claimed as their own, only to lose them when a stronger neighbor or a new ruler decided otherwise. What changed the story wasn't might–it was paper. A title deed, filed and recognized, turned dirt into property that courts would defend. The same is true today: shares in a company, patents, wills, trusts–each exists only because paper says so.

Paperwork may look dull, but it compounds. The person who keeps meticulous records of investments, expenses, and contracts has an advantage over the one who relies on memory. When disputes arise, the one with paper wins. When opportunities appear, the one with paper moves faster, because their affairs are already in order. Wealth grows in the spaces where clarity replaces ambiguity, and paperwork is clarity made permanent.

The irony is that paperwork feels optional until it isn't. Nobody cares about the unsigned agreement when things are going well. But the moment a deal sours, the absence of paper becomes catastrophic. That's when you discover that paperwork was never bureaucracy–it was your shield.

Paperwork is power because it transforms wealth from something informal and fragile into something formal and durable. Without it, you own only what others allow. With it, you own what the system itself protects.

## Rule 57 – Privacy is protection

In a world where information is currency, privacy is armor. The more others know about your finances, your plans, your weaknesses, the easier it becomes for them to exploit you. Wealth attracts attention, and attention attracts risk. Privacy is how you reduce that exposure.

Privacy doesn't mean secrecy for its own sake. It means controlling the flow of information. Deciding what to reveal, when, and to whom. The wealthy understand that visibility invites claims—tax authorities, competitors, opportunists, even family members. By keeping their affairs discreet, they reduce the number of people who can interfere with them.

The paradox is that modern life encourages oversharing. Social media trains people to broadcast their lifestyles, purchases, and locations. Companies encourage you to surrender data in exchange for convenience. Governments demand increasing transparency in the name of compliance. Against that tide, privacy looks old-fashioned. But the moment you lose it, you realize how valuable it was.

Privacy is also psychological protection. When your finances are not public, you feel less pressure to perform for others. You can live below your means without embarrassment, invest in boring assets without criticism, decline flashy opportunities without explanation. Privacy frees you from the comparisons that corrode judgment.

This is not about hiding wealth in shadows. It is about recognizing that exposure makes you fragile. Privacy is the margin of safety for your identity, your assets, and your decisions. Once it is gone, you cannot easily buy it back.

Privacy is protection because it shields you from a world eager to turn your visibility into their opportunity. Guard it as carefully as you guard your capital—because in the long run, they are the same thing.

## Rule 58 – Diversification is survival

Diversification is often reduced to a slogan: *don't put all your eggs in one basket.* But beneath the cliché lies a deeper truth: diversification is not about maximizing returns. It is about ensuring survival. The single biggest risk in wealth is not underperformance–it is ruin. And diversification is how you avoid ruin.

Imagine betting everything on one company, one property, one country, one idea. For a time, it may look brilliant. Concentration often produces the highest short-term gains. But it also creates fragility. If that one bet fails–and history suggests it eventually will–you don't just lose money. You lose the ability to stay in the game.

Survival is underrated because it's invisible. You don't notice the disasters you avoided. You don't celebrate the crises that never touched you. But avoiding ruin is the only way compounding can work, and compounding is the only reliable path to wealth. Diversification trades a little bit of upside for a lot of endurance, and endurance is what actually builds fortunes.

The psychology of diversification is difficult because it feels unsatisfying. Watching one investment skyrocket while your diversified portfolio lags behind is frustrating. You feel like you're missing out. But the cost of concentration is that when the story flips, you don't just miss out–you're destroyed. Diversification may look mediocre in the short term, but in the long term, it is what separates survivors from casualties.

Diversification is survival. And survival is victory, because the last investor standing is the one compounding gets to reward.

## Rule 59 – Complexity hides risk

Complexity has a way of making people feel safe. The more sophisticated the model, the more detailed the structure, the more clever the product, the more people assume risk is under control. But the opposite is usually true: complexity hides risk instead of eliminating it.

Consider the 2008 financial crisis. Wall Street packaged subprime mortgages into elaborate securities that almost no one fully understood. Ratings agencies blessed them with investment-grade labels. Investors assumed the complexity meant safety. In reality, the complexity hid fragility. When the system cracked, trillions vanished, and everyone acted shocked. The risks were always there—they were just buried under layers of jargon.

The same dynamic happens on a smaller scale every day. An investor buys a product they can't explain. A business launches operations with too many moving parts. A household finances a lifestyle with complicated loans. Complexity gives the illusion of control while making it harder to see where the weak points are.

Simple systems reveal risks. You can look at them and quickly spot what might go wrong. Complex systems bury those risks until it's too late. That is why the wealthy who endure often prefer boring clarity to exciting complexity. They would rather see their vulnerabilities clearly than hide them under structure.

Complexity is seductive because it flatters intelligence. It makes you feel smart to own something others don't understand. But fragility does not care about ego. When stress arrives, the complexity that once looked sophisticated collapses faster than the simple system that was built to be transparent.

The lesson is straightforward: complexity is not protection. It is camouflage. If you don't understand it, you're not diversified–you're blind.

## Rule 60 – Offshore is structure, not escape

When people hear the word *offshore*, they imagine secrecy: hidden accounts, tax evasion, or shadowy schemes. Hollywood built an entire mythology around the idea that moving money across borders is an act of escape. The reality is more mundane—and more powerful. Offshore is not escape. It is structure.

Wealthy individuals and businesses use offshore systems not to hide, but to organize. Different jurisdictions offer different rules on taxes, asset protection, inheritance, privacy, and corporate governance. By placing certain assets offshore, you are not running away—you are building a framework that protects wealth against the risks of a single country's laws or politics. Offshore is insurance against concentration.

Consider inheritance. In one country, estate taxes may claim half of what you leave behind. In another, trusts can preserve assets across generations with minimal disruption. Or consider business: in one jurisdiction, regulations may be unstable or biased. In another, company law may be predictable and investor-friendly. Offshore structures exist to take advantage of those differences.

The misconception comes from seeing offshore as a shortcut to avoid responsibility. In reality, the best offshore strategies are fully legal, fully transparent, and fully compliant. They don't replace discipline—they complement it. Offshore structures allow you to separate ownership from control, cash flow from liability, privacy from exposure. They are not magic, but architecture.

The irony is that offshore planning often looks boring. It's paperwork, registrations, compliance fees, and maintenance. Nothing cinematic. But boring is what you want in wealth preservation. Drama attracts attention, and attention attracts risk. Offshore done correctly is invisible, predictable, and robust.

Offshore is not an escape hatch for the reckless. It is scaffolding for the deliberate. If you see it as a way to run from problems, you will fail. If you see it as a way to design a system resilient to uncertainty, you will endure. Offshore is structure, not escape.

## Rule 61 – Jurisdictional arbitrage beats speculation

Speculation is gambling on what you cannot control. You buy a stock hoping it will rise. You bet on a currency hoping it will strengthen. Sometimes you're right, sometimes you're wrong. The outcome depends on forces larger than you. Jurisdictional arbitrage, on the other hand, is not about guessing markets. It is about choosing the rules you play under. And over time, that choice beats speculation almost every time.

Jurisdictional arbitrage means recognizing that different countries offer different systems—and that you are not obliged to accept the one you were born into. Some countries tax aggressively, others lightly. Some protect private property strongly, others weakly. Some make it easy to start businesses, others drown you in bureaucracy. By placing yourself, your business, or your assets under the jurisdiction with better rules, you tilt the game in your favor without betting on volatility.

Think of it as the difference between playing poker and choosing the table. At the poker table, you can win or lose depending on luck and skill. But if one table has a hidden rule that takes twenty percent of your winnings every hand, while another doesn't, the smart move is not to play harder—it's to switch tables. Jurisdictional arbitrage is switching tables.

Speculation is addictive because it promises quick gains. Jurisdictional arbitrage is boring because it feels administrative. But the returns of choosing the right jurisdiction compound silently. A business incorporated in a country with stable laws and low taxes outperforms the same business weighed down by hostile regulation. An investor who pays ten percent less in taxes every year ends up wealthier than the speculator who occasionally doubles their money but loses discipline.

The lesson is simple but uncomfortable: you don't need to outsmart the market if you can outsmart the map. Speculation makes you feel clever. Jurisdictional arbitrage makes you resilient. And resilience, over time, beats cleverness.

## Rule 62 – Every system has gatekeepers

No system is truly open. Behind every opportunity–whether it's access to capital, permits, markets, or influence–there are gatekeepers. These are the people, institutions, or mechanisms that decide who gets in and who stays out. They don't always wear badges or titles, but they hold the keys.

In finance, gatekeepers are regulators, banks, compliance officers, auditors. In business, they are licensing agencies, suppliers, distributors. In society, they are mentors, networks, even reputations. The myth of meritocracy tells us that talent alone wins. The reality is that gatekeepers filter talent, reward connections, and enforce rules, spoken or unspoken.

Understanding this changes how you approach wealth. Instead of assuming access is automatic, you begin asking: *Who controls this door? What do they value? How can I align with their incentives without compromising my principles?* Wealthy people don't just build businesses. They build relationships with the gatekeepers of their industries. They know that the right word from the right person opens doors that talent alone cannot.

The danger is ignoring gatekeepers. Believing rules don't apply to you, or that raw ability will bypass them, often leads to frustration or failure. History is full of brilliant innovators who couldn't commercialize their work because they underestimated the power of distribution networks, regulators, or cultural norms. Talent without access remains potential.

Gatekeepers are not obstacles to resent. They are fixtures to understand. Every system has them, and wealth flows to those who learn to navigate the gates instead of banging on them blindly.

## Rule 63 – Rules multiply in crisis

In calm times, systems tolerate ambiguity. Regulations stay light, oversight is lax, enforcement is forgiving. But in crises—wars, recessions, pandemics—rules multiply. Governments, institutions, and even companies respond to stress by creating layers of restrictions, reporting, and compliance. Each new rule is meant to stabilize the system. Together, they make it heavier and harder to move.

This is why crises create two kinds of people: those who collapse under the weight of new rules, and those who anticipated them. Businesses that thrived under light regulation often fail when governments tighten controls. Investors who ignored paperwork find themselves locked out when compliance suddenly matters. Citizens who never thought about residency or citizenship discover their mobility limited by border controls.

The psychology here is important. Rules born in crisis rarely disappear after it. They linger, because once a system expands authority, it rarely gives it back. The rules that multiply in crisis become the baseline of the new normal. What felt temporary becomes permanent.

For wealth, this means preparation. Assume that the next crisis—whatever its form—will bring more restrictions, not fewer. Have liquidity to weather freezes. Keep paperwork in order. Diversify across jurisdictions so one country's emergency rules don't trap your entire fortune. Crises are unpredictable, but the reaction is not: rules will multiply.

The irony is that rules are meant to create order, but too many create paralysis. Navigating wealth requires understanding that freedom in good times is conditional. It lasts only until the next shock convinces authorities to tighten their grip. Those who accept this reality prepare. Those who don't discover too late that the gates have already closed.

# Rule 64 – Governments protect themselves first

It's tempting to believe that governments exist to protect citizens. In practice, governments exist to protect themselves. Their survival—political, financial, institutional—always comes before your personal security. History proves this again and again.

When crises hit, governments act to preserve their own stability, even at the expense of individuals. In debt crises, they inflate away citizens' savings rather than default outright. In wars, they conscript young people to fight, not because it's good for families, but because it's necessary for the state. In financial collapses, they bail out institutions deemed "too big to fail," while households are left to endure.

This isn't cynicism. It's realism. A government cannot protect you if it cannot protect itself first. That hierarchy explains many policies that look unfair at the individual level but rational at the systemic level. It also explains why wealthy people diversify across borders: they don't assume one government will prioritize them forever.

The lesson is not distrust of all authority. The lesson is clarity. Understand that when trade-offs come, the state will choose its own continuity over your comfort. Plan accordingly. Hold assets in multiple jurisdictions. Keep liquidity outside systems that can be frozen. Build resilience that does not depend on one authority acting in your best interest.

Governments protect themselves first. If you accept this, you stop being surprised when laws shift, taxes rise, or freedoms shrink. You stop expecting fairness and start preparing for resilience.

## Rule 65 – Transparency has limits

We live in an age that worships transparency. Open data, radical disclosure, full visibility—these sound like virtues. And in many contexts, they are. Transparency reduces corruption, builds trust, and informs decisions. But transparency has limits. Beyond those limits, it becomes fragility.

Total transparency exposes you to exploitation. If competitors know your costs, they undercut you. If adversaries know your weaknesses, they exploit them. If the public sees every move, you lose the privacy necessary to experiment, fail, and learn. Even in personal finance, disclosing too much creates pressure to perform for others instead of for yourself.

The paradox is that transparency is good for systems, but dangerous for individuals. Governments push for more transparency from citizens—financial disclosures, digital footprints, reporting requirements—while protecting their own secrecy. Companies demand transparency from employees but guard their own strategies. The imbalance is not accidental. Transparency is power when imposed on others, and vulnerability when imposed on yourself.

The wealthy understand this. They practice selective transparency. They reveal enough to comply, to build trust, to operate legally. But they protect the core of their strategies, assets, and movements. They know that visibility creates targets, and invisibility creates resilience.

Transparency has limits because not all information deserves exposure. Some data protects you better in silence. Some moves are stronger in secrecy. The art is not choosing between transparency or secrecy, but knowing what belongs where.

## Rule 66 – Bureaucracy outlives regimes

Regimes fall. Leaders resign. Parties lose elections. Yet through all of it, one thing remains: the bureaucracy. The civil servants, administrators, clerks, regulators–these are the gears of the system, and they keep turning no matter who sits at the top.

This is why dealing with government often feels timeless. You may live through revolutions, policy shifts, even constitutional changes, but the forms remain, the procedures endure, the offices stay open. Bureaucracy is not loyal to ideology; it is loyal to its own survival. It creates rules, and then those rules create momentum. Once established, bureaucracies rarely shrink.

For wealth, this matters more than most people realize. You might think political instability or regime change will free you from obligations. In practice, the obligations survive. Taxes are still collected. Contracts are still enforced–or selectively ignored–by the same bureaucrats who were there before. The faces at the top may change, but the system beneath them persists, often stronger than before.

The irony is that bureaucracy is often ridiculed as inefficient. And yet, its inefficiency is precisely why it endures. It is slow to adapt, resistant to shocks, and indifferent to political cycles. For citizens, this can feel frustrating. For wealth planning, it is reality: regimes may collapse, but bureaucracy will still be standing, waiting for your paperwork.

If you want to build lasting wealth, don't just study politics. Study bureaucracy. Because bureaucracy, not ideology, is what will outlast you.

## Rule 67 – Data is property

In the industrial age, wealth was measured in land, factories, and capital. In the digital age, wealth is measured in data. Data is property–the raw material that powers businesses, governments, and entire economies. Yet most people treat it casually, giving it away for free in exchange for convenience.

Every click, purchase, and location ping is data. Companies collect it, process it, and monetize it. Governments demand it, regulate it, and sometimes weaponize it. Individuals ignore it, until they realize too late that their personal data has been sold, leaked, or stolen. The irony is that in an age where data is as valuable as gold, most people protect their wallets more fiercely than their information.

For wealth, data is leverage. Knowing what customers want before they do. Knowing where markets move before headlines catch up. Owning proprietary data sets is like owning land in the 1800s–it defines who controls the future. And just like land, data is subject to disputes, theft, and regulation.

The psychology here is subtle. Because data is invisible, people underestimate its value. You can hold cash. You can see land. Data feels abstract, so people dismiss it. But invisibility doesn't make it less powerful. In fact, it makes it easier to extract from the unguarded.

Treat your data as property. Protect it with the same seriousness you protect your financial accounts. Understand that what you reveal online is often more valuable to others than it is to you. And if you build wealth in the digital economy, remember: the strongest moats are not factories or patents—they are the unique data streams competitors cannot replicate.

Data is property. Own it, guard it, and use it wisely. Because in the twenty-first century, it may be the most important asset you control.

## Rule 68 – Institutions remember longer than individuals

People forget. They retire, they move on, they pass away. But institutions–banks, courts, tax authorities, universities–remember. Their archives, databases, and records outlive the people who created them. For wealth, this means your past is never fully gone.

An unpaid tax bill can resurface decades later. A lawsuit dismissed today may linger in court records to be unearthed by a future investigator. A default, a bankruptcy, a regulatory fine–all of it is etched into institutional memory. Individuals might forgive. Institutions rarely do.

The paradox is that institutions are often faceless, which makes them feel forgetful. You assume that because the officer you dealt with retired, the issue disappeared. But institutions don't rely on memory. They rely on files, records, and systems designed to preserve continuity. That is why wealth planning must account not just for people, but for the institutions that will outlive them.

This endurance can be an advantage, too. Institutions also preserve rights. A deed, a patent, or a trust recorded properly can be defended long after the original owner is gone. The same bureaucracy that frustrates with its rigidity also protects with its persistence.

The wealthy understand this duality. They know institutions can be relentless adversaries or dependable allies, depending on how you engage them. Ignore them, and you will find that their memory is longer than yours. Respect them, and you can use that memory to protect your legacy.

Institutions remember longer than individuals. And in wealth, memory is power.

# Rule 69 – Leverage magnifies both gains and losses

Leverage is seductive. It promises more with less—bigger positions, faster growth, amplified returns. Used wisely, it can accelerate wealth. Used recklessly, it can erase fortunes overnight. Because leverage doesn't discriminate. It magnifies in both directions.

The psychology of leverage is dangerous because the upside is visible and immediate, while the downside is hidden and delayed. Borrow money, and your portfolio grows faster—until markets turn, and you discover that losses are multiplied, too. Expand your business with debt, and revenue surges—until cash flow tightens, and repayment becomes impossible. Leverage makes you look brilliant in good times and reckless in bad.

History is filled with stories of leverage gone wrong. From hedge funds to homeowners, from empires to entrepreneurs, the pattern repeats: confidence grows, leverage increases, the system looks invincible—until one shock, one downturn, one miscalculation reveals how fragile it always was. Wealth built slowly can endure shocks. Wealth built on leverage can collapse in days.

This doesn't mean leverage is always bad. Used conservatively, it can unlock opportunities that would otherwise take decades. But the key is humility. The more leverage you use, the less margin for error you have. And error is not optional—it is inevitable. The wealthy who last treat leverage like fire: powerful in controlled doses, destructive when it spreads.

Leverage magnifies both gains and losses. That truth is simple, but often forgotten in the excitement of growth. The question is not whether leverage works—it always works. The question is whether you can survive the version of it that works against you.

## Rule 70 – Liquidity is oxygen

Wealth can exist in many forms: real estate, equity, private businesses, collectibles. But unless part of it is liquid—cash or assets that can be quickly converted into cash—your wealth is like a body holding its breath. It looks alive, but the moment a crisis hits, it suffocates. Liquidity is oxygen.

Crises don't give you time to sell your house or wait for a business to recover. They demand cash now—for payroll, for debt payments, for emergencies. Without liquidity, you are forced to sell illiquid assets at fire-sale prices, turning temporary stress into permanent loss. This is why fortunes collapse not because of lack of assets, but because of lack of liquidity.

Liquidity also provides freedom. It lets you act when opportunities appear. A market downturn that panics others becomes a buying chance if you have cash on hand. An investment requiring fast capital is accessible only to those who can move money quickly. Liquidity is not just a shield—it is also a weapon.

The psychology of liquidity is difficult because cash feels unproductive. When markets are booming, holding liquidity looks foolish. Friends brag about high returns while your cash earns little. But what they see as drag is actually resilience. Liquidity is invisible in good times, but priceless in bad.

The wealthy understand that oxygen is not optional. You don't hold liquidity because you plan to need it. You hold it because someday, without warning, you will. And when that day comes, liquidity is the difference between survival and suffocation.

# Rule 71 – Contracts are weapons

Most people see contracts as formalities–paperwork to satisfy lawyers. But contracts are more than agreements. They are weapons. They enforce rights, allocate risks, and decide outcomes long after memory fades and relationships sour. A well-drafted contract is a shield when you are attacked, and a sword when you must press your claim.

Contracts matter because trust is fragile. Even honest partners can disagree when money is involved. A handshake may preserve goodwill in good times, but in conflict, only a contract speaks with authority. Courts don't enforce intentions. They enforce what is written.

The wealthy understand this. They treat contracts not as bureaucratic burdens, but as tools of strategy. They use them to control succession through wills and trusts. They shape partnerships with clauses that anticipate betrayal. They protect capital with covenants that prevent reckless borrowing. Each clause is a brick in the fortress, designed not for when things go well, but for when they go wrong.

The psychology here is subtle. People resist contracts because they feel confrontational–"don't you trust me?" But contracts are not about mistrust. They are about clarity. They prevent misunderstandings, remove ambiguity, and align expectations. Without them, disputes escalate into chaos. With them, disputes become solvable, often without ever reaching a courtroom.

History shows that fortunes rise and fall on the strength of contracts. Empires of trade, marriages between dynasties, cross-border businesses–all relied on enforceable agreements. The side with better contracts usually won.

Contracts are weapons. If you treat them as paperwork, you walk into battle unarmed. If you treat them as strategy, you carry protection that outlasts any promise.

## Rule 72 – Family is the most fragile structure

We like to imagine family as the ultimate foundation—blood ties, unconditional support, bonds that money cannot break. And sometimes that is true. But history and experience show that family, when wealth is involved, is often the most fragile structure of all.

Money amplifies everything. In families, it can amplify love through generosity, shared projects, and security. But it can just as easily amplify envy, resentment, and conflict. Inheritance disputes have torn apart siblings who once seemed inseparable. Business partnerships between relatives have collapsed under the weight of blurred roles and unspoken expectations. Parents who thought they were helping children with money often created dependency instead of independence.

The fragility comes from mixing two forces: emotion and finance. Emotions make families powerful, but they also make them volatile. Money, by nature, demands clarity, boundaries, and rules. When the two collide, the results can be explosive.

The wealthy understand this paradox. They don't assume family harmony will survive wealth by default. They design structures—trusts, governance boards, family constitutions—that protect relationships from money and money from relationships. They separate roles: family members can be heirs without being managers, beneficiaries without being decision-makers. They build systems to handle what love alone cannot.

None of this diminishes the value of family. It elevates it. By protecting family from the corrosive effects of money, wealth can serve its true role: strengthening bonds across generations. But pretending family is immune to the stresses of wealth is denial. Family is the most fragile structure, and treating it as invincible is the surest way to see it break.

# Rule 73 – Advisors serve their own interests first

Advisors are necessary. Lawyers, bankers, consultants, accountants–no one builds wealth without help. But it is dangerous to forget one truth: advisors serve their own interests first.

This doesn't mean advisors are dishonest. It means they are human. A banker wants you to borrow because lending is profitable. A fund manager wants you to invest in their product because that is how they earn fees. A lawyer may encourage complexity because complexity requires more legal work. Even the most ethical advisors operate within incentives that don't always align perfectly with yours.

The wealthy who endure never outsource judgment completely. They listen, they learn, they consult–but they keep ultimate responsibility for decisions. They understand that no one cares about their wealth as much as they do. They pay for expertise, but they filter it through their own principles and long-term goals.

The danger of forgetting this rule is dependency. If you assume your advisor's advice is always in your best interest, you stop questioning, stop learning, and stop noticing when incentives diverge. Over time, that dependency erodes both capital and control.

Advisors are most valuable when you understand their incentives clearly. A good advisor can save you years of mistakes. A bad advisor–or even a good one whose incentives misalign–can undo decades of progress. The difference lies not just in their integrity, but in your awareness.

Advisors serve their own interests first. Respect that truth, and you will benefit from their knowledge without being captured by their incentives. Forget it, and you may discover too late that the fortune you built was fueling someone else's goals more than your own.

# Rule 74 – Save like a pessimist, invest like an optimist

The paradox of wealth is that it requires two mindsets that seem contradictory. You must save like a pessimist, but invest like an optimist. Saving demands you assume bad things will happen—layoffs, recessions, medical bills, accidents. Investing demands you assume good things will happen—growth, innovation, progress, recovery. If you confuse the two, you either hoard endlessly or gamble recklessly.

Saving like a pessimist means building cash buffers, buying insurance, and living below your means. It is admitting that the future is uncertain and that safety margins are not luxuries but necessities. Without pessimism in saving, you live exposed—one crisis away from collapse.

Investing like an optimist, on the other hand, means trusting that the future, despite setbacks, will trend upward. Markets rise because humanity solves problems over time. Economies grow because innovation compounds. To invest well, you must believe that even though tomorrow could be worse, the next decade will likely be better. Without optimism in investing, you never take the risks that compounding requires.

The tension between these two mindsets is what makes wealth hard. Most people lean too far one way: they either save so cautiously they miss growth, or they invest so aggressively they have nothing to fall back on. The wealthy who last balance both. They protect their downside with pessimism and pursue their upside with optimism.

Save like you expect disaster. Invest like you expect recovery. That combination feels unnatural, but it is the formula for resilience.

## Rule 75 – Automatic beats emotional

Discipline is fragile. It bends under stress, temptation, and fatigue. But automation is resilient. Once in place, it works without asking for willpower. That is why, in wealth, automatic always beats emotional.

Think of savings. If you wait to see what's left at the end of the month, emotions will intervene. You'll justify the purchase, delay the transfer, forget the plan. But if savings are automated–deducted from your paycheck before you see it–they happen whether you feel disciplined or not. Automation turns intention into inevitability.

The same applies to investing. If contributions are scheduled, you buy through fear, greed, boredom, and distraction. You don't have to time the market because the system does it for you. Automation removes your mood from the equation, and moods are the biggest threat to compounding.

The psychology here is simple but profound. We all like to believe we are rational. In reality, we are emotional, and emotions fluctuate daily. Automation acknowledges this weakness and designs around it. It assumes you will be tempted, distracted, or discouraged–and protects you from yourself.

Automation is not just efficiency. It is defense. It ensures that the boring, repetitive actions that build wealth actually happen. Over time, those small, automatic steps accumulate into results that no amount of sporadic effort can match.

Automatic beats emotional because systems endure where willpower fails. If you want wealth to outlast your moods, let the machines do the work.

# Rule 76 – Wealth is built in decades, lost in days

Wealth moves slowly in one direction and violently in the other. Building it takes decades of small, disciplined decisions–savings repeated, investments held, risks managed. Losing it often takes only one event, one panic, one overreach. That asymmetry is what makes wealth fragile, and what makes humility essential.

Consider compounding. Ten percent growth over thirty years feels boring in the short run but extraordinary in the long run. Each year adds to the last, snowballing quietly until the numbers look almost impossible. Yet all of that work can be undone by one reckless bet, one ignored risk, one crisis where you sold in fear. What took decades to build can vanish in days.

The psychology here is dangerous because the slowness of building and the speed of losing feel unfair. We tolerate boredom while compounding works, but we have little tolerance for sudden pain when losses arrive. That impatience pushes people into desperate moves that accelerate the collapse.

The lesson is not to fear loss but to respect it. Expect that setbacks will come and build margins so they don't erase you. Diversify not to maximize gains, but to minimize the chance of ruin. Survive the bad days so the good decades can do their work.

Wealth is not a sprint won by brilliance. It is a marathon won by survival. The slow, steady climb is the point. And the awareness that you could lose it quickly is what keeps you humble enough to protect it.

## Rule 77 – Guard your mornings

Time is the currency wealth cannot buy back. And mornings are its most valuable denomination. The hours after you wake are when your mind is clearest, your discipline highest, your energy least diluted. Guard them, because how you spend your mornings often decides how you spend your life.

The wealthy understand that money is not their scarcest resource–attention is. If you let others control your mornings–with emails, demands, or distractions–you start every day reactive instead of intentional. One reactive day blends into another, until years have passed and you wonder why you never made progress on what mattered.

Guarding your mornings doesn't mean rituals of perfection. It means choosing deliberately. Maybe you use them for exercise, reading, strategy, or simply quiet. The point is not what the ritual is, but that it is yours. Once mornings are consumed by noise, the rest of the day is already compromised.

History shows this in the habits of thinkers, entrepreneurs, and investors. Many of them credit their mornings–their solitude, their thinking time–as the foundation of their work. They knew that decisions about capital were really decisions about attention, and attention is sharpest before the world intrudes.

The psychology is simple: mornings feel ordinary, so people treat them carelessly. But ordinary hours compound. Guard your mornings, and you create space for clarity that shapes decades. Waste them, and no amount of money will buy them back.

# Rule 78 – Status symbols are debts in disguise

Status looks expensive because it is. The luxury car, the designer watch, the oversized house–they all project wealth. But in most cases, they project debt. Status symbols rarely come from surplus. They come from obligations: payments, loans, commitments that eat away at freedom month after month.

The psychology is simple: people want recognition. They want proof that they've "made it." A status symbol buys that recognition instantly, even if the price is years of repayment. But recognition fades quickly. The car becomes normal, the house becomes ordinary, the watch no longer impresses. The debt, however, remains.

Wealth is invisible because it shows up in freedom, in liquidity, in resilience. Status is visible because it shows up in objects. And the irony is that the more someone spends to display wealth, the less wealth they usually have. The symbols are not the sign of success–they are the invoice.

This doesn't mean you can't enjoy luxuries. It means enjoy them only when they come from surplus, not sacrifice. If buying the thing increases your stress instead of your freedom, it isn't wealth–it's debt in disguise.

True status is not what others see. It's what you can walk away from. The quiet person driving the ordinary car with no debt is usually wealthier than the one signaling success loudly. Status symbols attract attention, but freedom is what endures.

## Rule 79 – Never outsource decisions completely

Advice is valuable. Mentors, advisors, consultants–they bring perspective and knowledge you may not have. But advice is not responsibility. The final decisions are yours, and outsourcing them entirely is dangerous.

The psychology here is tempting: letting someone else decide feels easier. If things go wrong, you can blame them. If things go right, you can take credit. But in reality, no one cares about your future as much as you do. Advisors have incentives, biases, and blind spots. They may be competent, but they are not accountable for your life. You are.

Wealthy people use advisors, but they never surrender judgment. They listen, they question, they weigh alternatives. Then they decide. This is not arrogance–it is ownership. Without ownership, you drift from one recommendation to the next, building a fortune that reflects someone else's interests more than your own.

The irony is that outsourcing decisions can feel like professionalism–"I'm trusting the experts." But professionalism without responsibility is dependency. The more dependent you become, the weaker your instincts grow. When the advisor is gone, you are left vulnerable.

The goal is balance: trust expertise, but keep the steering wheel. Seek advice, but don't confuse advice with authority. Never outsource completely, because the cost of being wrong is yours to bear, not theirs.

Wealth without ownership of decisions is fragile. Wealth guided by informed but independent judgment is resilient.

## Rule 80 – Diversify mentors, not just assets

Most people understand diversification in money. Fewer apply it to wisdom. But ideas, like investments, are fragile if they come from only one source. Depending on a single mentor, advisor, or role model creates blind spots just as dangerous as putting your entire net worth into one stock.

Different mentors teach different things. One might show you discipline, another creativity, another resilience. One may embody caution, another boldness. Each perspective adds a layer of protection against narrow thinking. Just as diversified assets smooth out volatility, diversified mentors smooth out judgment.

The danger of relying on a single mentor is that you inherit their strengths but also their weaknesses. If they are overly cautious, you become timid. If they are overly aggressive, you absorb their risk. A portfolio of mentors balances those extremes.

The wealthy who last rarely credit a single influence. They draw from many—authors, teachers, colleagues, even rivals. They are willing to learn from anyone, not to copy them, but to add another voice to their internal debate. Wisdom grows not from agreement but from contrast.

Diversifying mentors doesn't mean collecting an entourage. It means building a library of perspectives you can call on when decisions are hard. Because just as a single investment can fail, so can a single worldview. Diversify mentors, and your judgment becomes resilient enough to endure what no single teacher could prepare you for.

## Rule 81 – Travel teaches value

Travel is often seen as leisure, but for wealth, it is education. Stepping into another country, another economy, another culture reveals truths no book or chart can. It teaches value by showing you contrast.

In one place, a dollar stretches far. In another, it barely buys a meal. In one country, opportunity feels abundant; in another, scarcity shapes every decision. Travel shows you that wealth is relative–that comfort in one place is luxury in another, and survival in one place is extravagance elsewhere.

The lesson is not just economic. Travel exposes you to how people live, what they prioritize, and how they solve problems with limited resources. You see families thriving with less, and others burdened despite more. It forces you to question assumptions about what is necessary, what is excessive, and what really creates satisfaction.

The wealthy who travel gain more than memories. They gain perspective. They understand arbitrage not just in currencies or taxes, but in lifestyles. They realize that moving across borders can multiply freedom or reduce costs. They see that resilience often comes from adaptability, not accumulation.

Travel teaches value because it reframes wealth. It strips away the illusion that your way is the only way. It shows you that money's power depends entirely on where, how, and with whom it is spent. And once you learn that, you begin to see wealth less as numbers in an account and more as choices in a world larger than your own.

## Rule 82 – Comparison is poison

Money is relative. You don't just measure it against your needs–you measure it against others. Your salary feels good until you hear what your colleague earns. Your house feels large until you visit your neighbor's. Your portfolio looks impressive until a friend brags about doubling theirs overnight. Comparison turns sufficiency into scarcity, no matter the numbers.

The poison of comparison is that it shifts the finish line. What once felt like "enough" becomes inadequate. Progress that should feel satisfying instead feels embarrassing. You stop measuring against your own goals and start measuring against someone else's scoreboard. The tragedy is that someone else is always ahead.

This is why even billionaires can feel poor. There is always a larger yacht, a bigger deal, a richer rival. Comparison is an infinite game with no winners–only exhaustion. The antidote is to step out of the game entirely. Define your own version of wealth, tied to freedom, security, or purpose, not to signals others can see.

Wealth without comparison feels like peace. Wealth with comparison feels like hunger that no meal can satisfy. The richest people are not those who won the race against others. They are those who stopped running it.

Comparison is poison because it corrupts the only definition of wealth that matters: *your own.*

## Rule 83 – Prepare for black swans

A black swan is an event no one predicted, that feels obvious only in hindsight. A war, a pandemic, a market crash, a political upheaval. These events are rare, but they shape history more than all the ordinary days combined. Wealth that ignores them is fragile. Wealth that prepares for them is resilient.

The difficulty is that you cannot predict black swans. You cannot know their timing, form, or trigger. But you can assume they will happen, and design your life to survive them. That means keeping liquidity, avoiding excessive leverage, diversifying across assets and borders, and maintaining flexibility in lifestyle and business. Survival is not about predicting shocks–it is about absorbing them.

Psychologically, black swans expose illusions of control. They remind us that models, forecasts, and plans are only as strong as the assumptions behind them. They humble even the most sophisticated players, because no one is exempt from uncertainty.

The wealthy who last are paranoid optimists. They believe in long-term progress, but they expect short-term chaos. They don't know what the next black swan will be, but they know it will come. And when it does, they don't need brilliance. They need margin.

Prepare for black swans not by fearing the unknown, but by building a structure that bends without breaking. The future will always surprise you. The question is not whether you can see it coming, but whether you can stand when it arrives.

## Rule 84 – True wealth survives its owner

Wealth is often measured in net worth while you are alive. But the truest measure is what happens after you are gone. Money that disappears when you die was income. Wealth that survives you was capital.

True wealth is not only what you built–it is what endures. Businesses that outlive founders, estates that support families across generations, endowments that fund causes long after the donor is gone. These are the marks of wealth that transcends mortality. Without that endurance, success ends when you do.

The psychology is humbling. We all like to believe we are central, that our decisions are what matter. But continuity requires systems, not personalities. If your wealth depends only on you, it dies with you. If it is embedded in structures–trusts, institutions, habits–it can live on.

The wealthy who last think in terms of stewardship, not ownership. They don't just ask, *how do I grow this?* They ask, *how do I make this survive me?* That shift–from possession to preservation–is what transforms fortune into legacy.

True wealth survives its owner. Anything else is just temporary success.

# Rule 85 – Inheritance without education is destruction

Passing money to heirs without passing wisdom is like handing a loaded weapon to someone who has never held one before. Inheritance can empower, but without education it almost always destroys.

The numbers are sobering: most family fortunes are gone by the third generation. Not because the money vanished on its own, but because the heirs were unprepared. They inherited capital without discipline, opportunity without perspective, abundance without gratitude. What was built through patience was lost through ignorance.

Education here doesn't mean formal schooling. It means teaching values: the discipline of saving, the fragility of wealth, the dangers of envy, the importance of purpose. It means showing heirs not just how to spend money, but how to manage, protect, and grow it. It means sharing not just assets, but the principles that made those assets possible.

The irony is that many parents avoid this conversation. They think shielding children from financial reality is kindness. In truth, it is negligence. Money without context overwhelms. It funds self-destruction faster than it funds opportunity.

Inheritance without education is destruction because money magnifies character. If heirs are disciplined, wealth empowers them. If they are careless, wealth accelerates their fall. The only way to tilt that equation is to make education part of the inheritance.

## Rule 86 – A name is more fragile than money

Money can be rebuilt after loss. A name often cannot. Once reputation is damaged, it follows you like a shadow–hard to escape, impossible to fully erase. That is why a family name, a company name, or even your personal name is often more fragile than the wealth attached to it.

History is filled with fortunes that were squandered, only to be rebuilt in the next generation. But when a name becomes synonymous with scandal, corruption, or betrayal, it rarely recovers. Banks collapse but reopen under new brands. Families relocate but carry the stigma with them. Money can be laundered. A name cannot.

The fragility comes from trust. Your name is shorthand for whether people believe you will keep your word, honor commitments, or act fairly. Trust takes decades to build, but one careless act can stain it permanently. A reckless lawsuit, a public humiliation, a breach of integrity–these can outlast all financial mistakes.

Wealthy families who endure treat the name as an asset to be protected more fiercely than any account. They avoid short-term gains that could leave long-term scars. They remind heirs that their choices do not just affect themselves, but everyone who carries the same name.

A name is not on the balance sheet, but it is the foundation of every deal, partnership, and opportunity. Protect it as if it were the most valuable asset you own–because it is.

## Rule 87 – Legacy is continuity, not monuments

When people think of legacy, they imagine monuments: buildings named after them, foundations carved in stone, speeches honoring their lives. But true legacy is not what people remember. It is what continues.

Legacy is continuity. It is systems that endure beyond your presence–businesses that keep running, families that stay united, principles that guide decisions long after you are gone. A monument may crumble. A habit may last forever.

The mistake many make is confusing visibility with impact. They fund monuments that look impressive but serve no real purpose. Meanwhile, the quiet investments–education for heirs, governance structures for family wealth, endowments for causes–shape the future in ways that outlast recognition.

The wealthy who endure think less about how they will be remembered and more about how the structures they built will function without them. They don't ask, *Will people know my name?* They ask, *Will people still benefit from my work?* That shift in focus changes everything.

Legacy as continuity is humbler, quieter, and stronger. It doesn't seek applause. It seeks endurance. And endurance is the only legacy worth leaving.

## Rule 88 – Freedom is designed, not granted

Most people think freedom is something handed down–by governments, by employers, by circumstances. But waiting for freedom to be granted is the surest way to never have it. Real freedom is not a gift. It is a structure you build.

Freedom is designed through choices: saving when it would be easier to spend, saying no when it would be easier to conform, building margins when it would be easier to stretch. Each choice feels small in the moment, even restrictive. But together, they form an architecture of independence. Without that design, freedom is just a word on paper–available in theory, absent in practice.

The psychology of freedom is paradoxical. To outsiders, it looks effortless. Someone who can walk away from a toxic job or decline a bad deal seems lucky. But what they see as luck is actually design–years of preparation, discipline, and foresight. Freedom looks spontaneous only because the work that created it was invisible.

The danger is believing freedom will arrive automatically once you have "enough." But enough never defines itself. If you don't design the terms of your independence, someone else will. Employers, governments, creditors, even family will shape your life around their interests. Freedom requires intention, not assumption.

The wealthy who endure understand this. They don't wait for freedom to be granted. They write contracts that preserve it. They build liquidity that defends it. They design lives where obligations never grow faster than choices. They accept that sovereignty is not inherited–it is engineered.

Freedom is designed, not granted. If you don't build it, you will spend your life negotiating for it.

# Final words

Wealth is a paradox. It is both simple and complex, fragile and resilient, visible and invisible. People chase it across lifetimes, convinced it is about money, only to discover—often too late—that money was only the surface. Wealth is rhythm, patience, discipline, and above all, survival.

This book began with simple foundations: save before you spend, live below your means, protect before you grow. These ideas sound ordinary, but ordinariness is the point. Extraordinary results are built from ordinary actions repeated across decades. It is tempting to believe wealth requires brilliance or secrets. In truth, it requires endurance.

From there, we entered psychology—the battlefield where most fortunes are won or lost. Fear, greed, envy, overconfidence: these forces shape behavior far more than data or forecasts. Investors don't fail because they lack intelligence. They fail because they cannot sit still, cannot ignore comparison, cannot resist the urge to chase shortcuts. The hardest part of money is never the math. It is the emotions.

Then we turned to systems and structures—the external rules that govern opportunity. Laws shift. Borders matter. Institutions remember longer than individuals. Bureaucracies outlive regimes. Wealth cannot ignore these truths. You do not operate in a vacuum. You operate inside structures that can protect or destroy you depending on how well you understand them. Money without structure is sand. Money within structure is stone.

Discipline and practice followed: the habits that quietly determine whether wealth compounds or crumbles. Automation beats emotion. Black swans arrive. Comparison is poison. Save like a pessimist, invest like an optimist. These are not tactics. They are temperaments. They are the way you carry yourself through decades of uncertainty. Without discipline, even the best structures collapse.

Finally, we arrived at continuity and legacy. Wealth is not what you spend, and not even what you hold. It is what survives you. True wealth is the business that outlasts its founder, the inheritance paired with education, the name preserved with integrity, the systems that continue long after you are gone. Legacy is not a monument. It is continuity.

Threaded through all of this is one theme: freedom. Freedom is not granted. It is designed. Every rule in this book points to that truth. You design freedom when you save first, when you control expenses, when you automate decisions, when you diversify across borders, when you protect your family with clarity instead of assumptions. Freedom is the architecture built from thousands of small, unglamorous decisions. It looks invisible until the day you need it.

The world will always tempt you otherwise. Headlines will scream fear. Crowds will chant greed. Advisors will serve their own interests first. Governments will protect themselves before they protect you. The illusion of certainty will seduce you. The pressure to compare will poison you. If you forget these truths, you will confuse noise for signal and end up building a fortune too fragile to last.

But if you remember–if you internalize that wealth is not brilliance but survival, not speed but patience, not status but freedom–then you will live differently. You will design your structures with humility. You will protect your mornings, your liquidity, your reputation. You will pass on education with inheritance. You will measure wealth not in symbols, but in choices.

And when the day comes that you are no longer here, your wealth will not vanish. It will survive–not because you hoped, but because you designed it that way.

The final truth is this: wealth is rhythm, not a destination. It is the rhythm of restraint, of protection, of patience, of design. Follow the rhythm long enough, and the freedom others wait to be granted will already be yours.

## Thank You Note

Thank you for spending your time with this book. Writing it has been a way to put into words the lessons I've seen play out over years–not in theory, but in real life, in courtrooms, boardrooms, and families trying to make sense of money.

If one rule or one story here has helped you see money differently, then this book has done its job. My hope is not that you remember all 88 rules, but that a few of them stay with you at the right moments–when fear, greed, or pressure tempt you to forget what really matters.

Wealth is not about chasing numbers. It's about building freedom, protecting what you care about, and passing on something that lasts. If these pages have brought you a little closer to that, I'm grateful.

So thank you—for reading, for thinking, and for choosing to invest in ideas that may outlast trends, headlines, and even us.

—Mia Galgau

*Thank you.*

**Technical and Copyright Information**
**Title:** *The 88 Rules of Wealth*
**Author:** Mia Galgau
**Publisher:** Taxhells.com
**First Edition:** 2025


This book is published for educational purposes. It is not legal, financial, or tax advice. Readers should always consult qualified professionals before acting on decisions that affect their legal, financial, or personal situation. Laws and regulations evolve, and their application varies by jurisdiction. While care has been taken to provide accurate and current information, neither the author nor the publisher can guarantee its applicability in the future or accept responsibility for the use of this material.

Thank you.

www.ingramcontent.com/pod-product-compliance
Lightning Source LLC
LaVergne TN
LVHW101502200926
848483LV00001B/203